CHAMPIONS OF FREEDOM

The Ludwig von Mises Lecture Series

CHAMPIONS OF FREEDOM
Volume 35

America's
Entitlement Society

Hillsdale College Press
Hillsdale, Michigan 49242

Hillsdale College Press

CHAMPIONS OF FREEDOM
The Ludwig von Mises Lecture Series—Volume 35
America's Entitlement Society

©2008 Hillsdale College Press, Hillsdale, Michigan 49242

First printing 2008

The views expressed in this volume are not necessarily the views of Hillsdale College.

Printed in the United States of America

Front cover: Fistful of Money, Open Hands by Sandra Dionisi © Corbis

Library of Congress Control Number: 2008924126

ISBN-13 978-0-916308-05-7

Contents

Contributors

Larry P. Arnn is the twelfth president of Hillsdale College. He received his B.A. from Arkansas State University and his M.A. and Ph.D. in government from the Claremont Graduate School. He also studied at the London School of Economics and at Worcester College, Oxford University. From 1985 to 2000, he was president of the Claremont Institute for the Study of Statesmanship and Political Philosophy. He is on the boards of directors of the Heritage Foundation, the Henry Salvatori Center at Claremont McKenna College, Americans Against Discrimination and Preferences, the Center for Individual Rights, and the Claremont Institute. Dr. Arnn is the author of *Liberty and Learning: The Evolution of American Education*.

Doug Bandow is Vice President of Policy for Citizen Outreach, a Washington-based grassroots political organization. He received his B.S. in economics from Florida State University and his J.D. from Stanford University. He is the Bastiat Scholar in Free Enterprise at the Competitive Enterprise Institute and the Cobden Fellow in International Economics at the Institute for Policy Innovation. Formerly a senior fellow at the Cato Institute, he also served as a special assistant to President Ronald Reagan and as a senior policy analyst in the 1980 Reagan for President campaign. He has appeared on numerous radio and television programs and has been widely published in such newspapers and periodicals as the *New York Times*, *The Wall Street Journal*, *Time*, *Newsweek*, and *National Review*. Mr. Bandow has written and edited several books, including *Leviathan Unchained: Washington's Bipartisan Big Government Consensus*.

Herman Cain earned a degree in mathematics from Morehouse College and a master's degree in computer science from Purdue University while working as a mathematician for the Department of the Navy. He went on to work at the Coca-Cola Company and became Vice President of Corporate Systems and Services at the Pillsbury Company. He has also been a regional manager in Pillsbury's Burger King division and president of the Godfather's Pizza chain. A former chairman of the board of directors of the National Restaurant Association, he has also served on the Economic Growth and Tax Reform Commission and as chairman and member of the board of directors for the Federal Reserve Bank of Kansas City. A senior advisor to the 1996 Dole presidential campaign and a member of the National Rifle Association board of directors, he is also CEO and president of Retail-DNA. He serves on the boards of directors for Hallmark Cards and Whirlpool Corporation. In 2004, he ran as a candidate for the United States Senate from Georgia. A nationally syndicated radio talk show host and a FOX News business commentator, Mr. Cain is the author most recently of *They Think You're Stupid: Why Democrats Lost Your Vote and What Republicans Must Do to Keep It*.

Jonathan Hoenig is the Managing Member of Capitalistpig Hedge Fund LLC, a private investment partnership he started in 2000. A former floor trader at the Chicago Board of Trade, his first book, *Greed is Good: The Capitalistpig Guide to Investing*, was published by Harper Collins and named one of *Money Magazine*'s Best Business Books of 1999. An advocate of free market capitalism, he is a frequent commentator in the financial press and has written for publications including *The Wall Street Journal Europe*, *Wired*, *Trader Monthly*, *Maxim*, and Smartmoney.com. He has been featured in numerous publications including *The Wall Street Journal*, *Institutional Investor*, *Fast Company*, and *The Chronicle of Higher Education*, and appears regularly on the FOX News Channel. Mr. Hoenig was named one of the *Chicago Sun-Times'*

"Thirty Under Thirty" and *Crain*'s "Forty Under Forty," and is a member of the Economic Club of Chicago.

John Marini, a professor in the department of political science at the University of Nevada, Reno, is a graduate of San Jose State and earned his Ph.D. in government at the Claremont Graduate University. He has also taught at Agnes Scott College, Ohio University, and the University of Dallas. During the Reagan administration, he served as a special assistant to Justice Clarence Thomas, who was then the chairman of the Equal Employment Opportunity Commission. He is a member of the board of the Claremont Institute, and a member of the Nevada Advisory Committee of the U.S. Civil Rights Commission. Dr. Marini is the author of several popular and scholarly articles on politics and political science, and the author or editor of numerous books, including *The Progressive Revolution in Politics and Political Science: Transforming the American Regime*; *The Imperial Congress: Crisis in the Separation of Powers*; and *The Politics of Budget Control: Congress, the Presidency, and the Growth of the Administrative State*.

Stephen Moore is senior economics writer for *The Wall Street Journal* editorial page and a member of the *Journal*'s editorial board. He is a graduate of the University of Illinois and holds an M.A. in economics from George Mason University. Previously, he served as founder and president of the Club for Growth. He has also served as a senior fellow in economics at the Cato Institute, where he published numerous studies on federal budget and tax policy. An economics commentator for CNBC, he is also a frequent guest on CNN and FOX News Channel. He has also served as a senior economist at the Joint Economic Committee under former Chairman Dick Armey of Texas, worked for two presidential commissions, and was research director for President Reagan's commission on privatization. Mr. Moore is the author of four books, including *It's Getting Better All the Time: The 100 Greatest Trends of the Last Century* and *Bullish on Bush: How the Ownership Society Will Make America Stronger*.

Charles Murray, the W. H. Brady Scholar at the American Enterprise Institute, received his B.A. in history from Harvard University and his Ph.D. in political science from the Massachusetts Institute of Technology. He has been a fellow with the Manhattan Institute, has worked for the American Institutes for Research, and spent six years in Thailand, first as a Peace Corps volunteer, then as a researcher in rural Thailand. In addition to technical journals, he has published in the *Atlantic*, *The New Republic*, *Commentary*, *The Wall Street Journal*, *National Review*, and *The Washington Post*, among others. He has been a witness before congressional and Senate committees and worked as a consultant to senior government officials of the United States, England, and Eastern Europe. He has been a frequent guest on major network news and public affairs programs. Dr. Murray's books include *Losing Ground: American Social Policy 1950–1980*; *The Bell Curve: Intelligence and Class Structure in American Life* (with Richard J. Herrnstein); *What It Means to be a Libertarian: A Personal Interpretation*; and, most recently, *In Our Hands: A Plan to Replace the Welfare State*.

Foreword

This is the 35th volume of *Champions of Freedom*, a book series that collects the papers delivered at Hillsdale College's annual Ludwig von Mises lectures. The essays in this volume, delivered in January 2007, center on the theme of entitlements in American society.

For the second consecutive year, we note the passing of a friend. Suzanne Dettwiler died this May at the age of 92. Mrs. Dettwiler and her late husband, Herman "Dett" Dettwiler, were devoted friends of the cause of freedom. Neither this book series nor the lecture series from which it draws could have existed without their generous support. We dedicate this volume, then, to her memory.

LARRY P. ARNN
President
Hillsdale College
November 2007

Acknowledgments

Special thanks to the
PHILIP M. MCKENNA FOUNDATION
LATROBE, PENNSYLVANIA
and to the
RICHARD E. FOX CHARITABLE FOUNDATION
STEAMBOAT SPRINGS, COLORADO
for their sponsorship of this volume

Introduction

In the movie, *Cinderella Man*, James Braddock falls on hard times as a boxer during the Great Depression and has to go on the federal dole. Later in the movie, when he has secured some fights and is on his way to becoming the heavyweight champion of the world, he returns to the welfare line and gives back all the money that he had received. This scene is startling because we could not imagine anyone doing so today. The reason is that Lyndon Johnson's Great Society created an enormous shift in the American attitude about government assistance. During Braddock's time, government assistance was something that you refrained from using unless absolutely necessary, and you were grateful for its existence. Today, welfare, along with Social Security, Medicaid, Medicare, public education, and hundreds of federal programs are seen as entitlements. While seemingly subtle, this change in attitude is profound and affects our view of personal responsibility and the role of government.

The New Deal began many federal programs, but until the 1960s the average American had not come to rely on them for his security. With the advent of The Great Society, Americans were told that they were entitled to the federal benefits from these programs, and that they should actively seek them out rather than avoid them. The old moral constraint on taking advantage of what Frederic Bastiat called "false philanthropy" was pushed aside.[1] In 1850, Basitiat warned that a government engaged in philanthropy could not be limited in its power, as there are an infinite number of cases of need for assistance. Today, millions of recipients of Social Security, Medicare, federal housing programs, disaster assistance relief, and every other example of government taking from one person to give to another, don't recognize these programs for what they are—in the words of Bastiat, legalized plunder. This forms the foundation of America's Entitlement Society.

This change in Americans' view of the welfare state also altered our view of individual responsibility. We are no longer responsible for taking care of our parents in their old age, or taking care of the impoverished or homeless, or for where we place our house or how our children are educated. In 1960, Nobel Laureate Friedrich Hayek wrote: "Our whole attitude toward the working of our social order, our approval or disapproval of the manner in which it determines the relative position of different individuals, is closely tied up with our views about responsibility."[2] The advent of the entitlement society began the decline of belief in individual responsibility and with it a reduction in our individual liberty. For, as Hayek also pointed out: "Liberty and responsibility are inseparable."[3]

The essays in this volume examine, from a practical side and from a philosophical side, the current state of the federal government's redistribution of wealth in its various forms. The authors make the point that the entitlement society in its various forms is a threat to our liberty, and that the promises made on the part of our government and the subsequent expectations of the populace are not sustainable within a free society.

President Arnn's essay addresses the issue of higher education. He points out that education was recognized to be of utmost importance to the Founders and that no less a figure than George Washington pressed for a national university. Yet the early Congress stood by the Constitution in finding that Article 8 did not provide the federal government with an enumerated power to deal with education. Dr. Arnn continues with a careful analysis of the nation's early views on education and makes a clear argument that education is not a right in the same fashion as free speech or peaceable assembly. He then documents America's slide into confusion over this issue, joined by the United Nations General Assembly. The conclusion we are drawn to is that the idea of a right or an entitlement to education is actually destructive to education itself.

Doug Bandow looks at the history and track record of America's largest entitlement program, Social Security, beginning with its roots in nineteenth-century Germany, noting it was Otto von Bismark who "hit upon the idea of making German citizens dependent on the state." Mr. Bandow goes on to show that much the same philosophy was behind President Roosevelt's Social Security program. He examines the economics of the Social Security progam and its sister, Medicare, and finds that these programs are simply not sustainable. His conclusion is that there is one politically viable solution to this Ponzi scheme—the introduction of private accounts along with a return to the idea that we, not the government, are responsible for our retirement.

Herman Cain's paper focuses on the relationship between entitlement and opportunity. His discussion ranges across several concepts and issues, including happiness, liberty, and inalienable rights. A major concern of Mr. Cain is the effect of an entitlement mentality on the nation. After tracing the origins of the entitlement mentality, he makes the argument that education is the key to returning to the concept the Founders espoused, or what he calls the opportunity mentality.

Jonathan Hoenig uses the analogy of the trader to explain the problems posed by an entitlement mentality. He emphasizes the importance to society of its citizens being held responsible for their actions. Mr. Hoenig provides examples of the entitlement mentality among groups that are often associated with free markets and individual responsibility. He examines the benefits of what Schumpeter called the "creative destruction" of modern capitalism. Interestingly, he claims that altruism is incompatible with individual liberty. This is at odds with the views of Bastiat and Hayek. In particular, Hayek wrote: "The freedom to pursue one's owns aims (which he defines as liberty) is, however, as important to the most altruistic person, in whose scale of values the needs of other people occupy a very high place, as for any egoist. . . . Moral esteem would be meaningless without freedom."[4] The careful reader may be able to reconcile these views.

John Marini, through judicious use of selections from their speeches, draws a clear distinction between the views of government held by Franklin Roosevelt and Ronald Reagan. The former justified the administrative state and the latter attempted to re-limit government. Roosevelt, the architect of the welfare state, viewed government as the provider of economic security, and posited that Americans had rights to jobs and goods and services, such as education and health care. Dr. Marini contrasts Roosevelt's understanding with that of the Founders. He then analyzes the attempt by Ronald Reagan to return the country to its original view of a limited government under a written Constitution, showing how Reagan restored belief in individual liberty and individual responsibility.

Steven Moore asks what happened to the Republican Revolution that sparked the Contract with America. His answer is that Republicans lost their "brand"—standing as the party of limited government, lower taxes, and fiscal responsibility. One example Mr. Moore provides is the fact that under the first six years of the Bush administration the Department of Education was the fastest growing department, doubling its spending. He then shows how the government's reaction to Hurricane Katrina was to create a hurricane of spending tax dollars. This spending, he argues, actually depressed the efforts of private charities, and the entire situation would have been better handled had the federal government not engaged in such false philanthropy. Moore concludes that the entitlement mentality of Americans has worked to create bureaucracies of waste and dampened the fire of individual and community charity that once graced our nation.

Charles Murray makes the case for revamping our entire federal system of income redistribution. He describes the reasoning behind the institution of the federal welfare state and points out its unintended consequences. He shows how the welfare state will change over time, becoming ever more destructive of our culture. But believing that the dismantling of the welfare state is not politically feasible, he proposes a negative income tax—something proposed in print by Milton Friedman in *Capitalism and Freedom* more than 40 years ago, and suggested much earlier by Friedman in correspondence with George Stigler. Dr. Murray outlines how this plan would be implemented, its feasibility, and the benefits that would ensue—in particular, the change in behavior of what has become known as the underclass.

The authors in this volume are concerned with more than just the cost and inefficiency of America's vast income transfer program. Their primary concern is the effect of the system of "false philanthropy" on the attitudes and behavior of Americans. Unlike true philanthropy, which benefits both parties, government transfer programs lead people to believe that the recipients of these programs are "entitled" to them. Each author points out problems that will develop when this mentality becomes endemic. The conclusion reached is the same one that Bastiat came to in 1850: The solution to social problems lies in individual liberty.

Notes

1. Frederic Bastiat, *The Law* (1850), trans. Dean Russell (Irvington-on-Hudson, NY: The Foundation for Economic Education, Inc., 1998).
2. Friedrich Hayek, *The Constitution of Liberty* (Chicago: University of Chicago Press, 1960).
3. Ibid.
4. Ibid.

HERMAN CAIN

Opportunity or Entitlement?

Dr. Benjamin Elijah Mays, late president of Morehouse College, used to challenge the young men of his school by saying, "It must be borne in mind that the tragedy of life does not lie in not reaching your goal. The tragedy in life lies in having no goal to reach." It is not a calamity to die with dreams unfulfilled, but it is a calamity to have no dreams. It is not a disaster to be unable to capture your ideals, but it is a disaster to have no ideals to capture.

Our Founding Fathers created this nation based upon the belief that "all men are created equal." The Declaration of Independence teaches that we have the rights to life, liberty, and the pursuit of happiness. We are not guaranteed happiness. Happiness is not an entitlement. Happiness depends on each individual's aspiration, motivation, and determination.

Steve Forbes, former presidential candidate, president and CEO of Forbes, and editor-in-chief of *Forbes* magazine, pointed something out to me that makes all the sense in the world about these principles of life, liberty and the pursuit of happiness. He said that in America you can pursue happiness as long as you don't infringe on someone else's liberty. You can have all the liberty that this country has to offer—as long as you don't infringe upon somebody else's life.

Martin Luther King defended inalienable rights. Dr. King proposed that we judge our fellow citizens by the content of their character and not the color of their skin. Unfortunately some people have forgotten that. They demand preferential treatment based on

1

skin color. They demand an entitlement. But this nation was founded on rights, not entitlements.

I believe that too many people in this country have an entitlement attitude. How did we get into a situation where so many people think that ours is an entitlement society, rather than an opportunity society?

It started in 1935 with Social Security, which was a well-intended assistance program. It was designed to assist people in their golden years. Every person working would contribute 3 percent of the first $3,000 of earnings to the Social Security program and the employer would contribute another 3 percent on the first $3,000 of income. The founders of the program insisted that this would be the most anyone would pay.

Today, instead of 3 percent, it is 7.65 percent paid by the employee and 7.65 percent paid by the employer on the first $94,200 of earnings. There are those in Congress who believe that the $94,200 cap should be eliminated, so that no matter what your income is, you pay 7.65%—on everything you make. Why? Because there are some who believe in promoting class warfare in this country, and this is one way to do it.

Social Security started as an assistance program, but since its inception it has grown exponentially and been transformed into an entitlement program. There is a structural problem with Social Security: More is being spent on benefits than is taken in as revenue. If it is not reformed, the Social Security system will collapse sometime in the next decade or so, 2017 or 2018. Yet there are those in Washington, DC, who are in denial.

Once begun, government programs always seem to cost more than promised. Consider the prescription drug plan that was passed recently by, I should note, a Republican Congress. The prescription drug plan was supposed to cost just short of $400 billion dollars over the next ten years. But before the ink had dried, its cost had gone up to $530 billion. Before the program was implemented, the new estimate was over $900 billion. Remember how it all started with Social Security? We were told that 3 percent on $3,000 was the most we would ever have to pay.

Social Security has become an entitlement program that is dysfunctional. When the president proposed a solution to fix the structure of the program, the Republican Congress did not have the courage to follow him. This allowed the bill's opponents to demagogue the idea, and the proposal failed. The lesson is that there are people in this country who believe we live in an entitlement society and regardless of how dysfunctional Social Security is, they don't believe we should fix it.

Consider Medicare, which began in 1965 as an assistance program to help older people deal with health-care costs. When Medicare was first rolled out, its costs were estimated at $6 billion. When it was passed, the public was told that in 25 years (by the year 1990) the cost would double. The actual recorded cost in 1990 was $109 billion, which means the program's founders underestimated its cost by 900 percent. As a result, Medicare is headed for a train wreck.

There are some who aspire to be president of the United States who talk about universal health care. They give the impression that it is not going to cost anybody anything. They ignore all of the evidence from nations that have socialized medicine—and make no mistake—universal health care is socialized medicine. Talk to someone from Canada. You may have heard stories about people who had to wait six months for a CT scan. But you won't see those stories on the nightly news.

The entitlement attitude is a disease. If someone is in denial, it is difficult to fix that. We are not going to be able to convert everybody, but we can convert some. It starts with education. People must see that their dreams are short-lived when they depend upon the government to make them happen.

In the 1980s, when I was president and CEO of Godfather's Pizza in Omaha, Nebraska, liberals in Congress were fighting to increase the minimum wage. A newspaper reporter wanted to interview me about it. At Godfather's we had 12,000 employees, and 8,000 were teenagers. I would guess half of them were on hourly wages and 33 percent were paid minimum wage. I was trying to explain to the reporter the ripple effect of government mandating any sort of price increase on businesses. Ultimately business must recoup that cost, which means the consumer is going to pay for it. Then the reporter asked: "What do you say to someone trying to support a family of four on minimum wage?" I looked her in the eye and said, "Don't. Don't try to support a family on minimum wage. Do what my Dad did. If one minimum wage job was not enough, he got two minimum wage jobs. If two minimum wage jobs were not enough, he got three minimum wage jobs. He did this until he got one good job, and didn't have to work three jobs. That is what you tell the person working on minimum wage."

What keeps people trapped in an entitlement attitude? Class warfare rhetoric and race warfare rhetoric are two big reasons. The American economy is strong. Yet there are some elected officials who say that this economy is headed in the wrong direction. The stock market has hit all-time highs, but there are some elected officials who will say that this stock market is not helping the middle-class, that it is not helping the little guy. Why? Because saying so fans the flames of class warfare. Our vibrant economy has produced a 4.5 percent unemployment rate, half that of most European countries. Millions of people have jobs because unemployment is so low, but all we hear in the mainstream media is that the middle class isn't benefiting from this economy.

Liberals believe that government should pass regulations in order to try and close what they perceive as a wealth gap. For example, they want government to control CEO pay. But when government tries to dictate to businesses what to pay employees, whether the CEO or the receptionist, we no longer have a free-market system. What we have instead is socialism.

As Ludwig Von Mises said, "Government cannot make a man richer, but government can make a man poorer." This is what would happen if we allowed government to micromanage the greatest economic engine in the world. Yet there are some people who do not understand this fundamental lesson of economics. And there are politicians who will pander to that. This class warfare rhetoric encourages the entitlement mentality.

Today's so-called civil rights leaders promote the entitlement mentality by fanning the flames of race relations. They blame minority failures, whether justified or not, on racism. But they don't understand that equal opportunity does not yield equal results. Today's civil rights leaders, such as Jesse Jackson or Al Sharpton, want to legislate results and outcomes. They don't understand that giving two people the same education and the same job does not guarantee that they are going to produce the same results. Thinking that this will happen leads to an entitlement attitude.

Remember, our nation is founded on rights, not on entitlements. The only way we are going to cure the entitlement disease is through education. It is hard work, and change will not happen over night. But we must keep trying. We must teach our fellow citizens that equal opportunity does not yield equal results. Ours is an ownership society, an opportunity society, not an entitlement society. We should not allow those who pander to people's fears and weaknesses to have the last word. This is our challenge as a nation, and therefore our greatest opportunity.

JOHN MARINI

Roosevelt's or Reagan's America?
A Time for Choosing

On January 11, 1944, President Franklin D. Roosevelt sent the text of his Annual Message to Congress. Under normal conditions, he would have delivered the message in person that evening at the Capitol. But he was recovering from the flu, and his doctor advised him not to leave the White House. So he delivered it as a fireside chat to the American people.

It has been called the greatest speech of the century by Cass Sunstein, a prominent liberal law professor at the University of Chicago. It is an important speech because it is probably the most far-reaching attempt by an American president to legitimize the administrative or welfare state, based on the idea that government must guarantee social and economic security for all.

Thirty-seven years later, in his First Inaugural Address, on January 20, 1981, President Ronald Reagan would deny that government could provide such a broad guarantee of security in a manner consistent with the protection of American liberty. Indeed, he would insist that bureaucratic government had become a danger to the survival of our freedom.

In looking at the differences between the views of Roosevelt and Reagan, we can discern the distinction between a constitutional regime—in which the power of government is limited so as to enable the people to rule—and an administrative state, which presupposes the rule of a bureaucratic or intellectual elite.

FDR's New Bill of Rights

When Roosevelt spoke to the nation that January night, he was looking beyond the end of World War II. In recent years, he said,

> Americans have joined with like-minded people in order to defend ourselves in a world that has been gravely threatened with gangster rule. But I do not think that any of us Americans can be content with mere survival. Sacrifices that we and our Allies are making impose upon us all a sacred obligation to see to it that out of this war we and our children will gain something better than mere survival.

And what was this "sacred obligation?" Roosevelt continued:

> The one supreme objective for the future, which we discussed for each nation individually, and for all the United Nations, can be summed up in one word: Security. And that means not only physical security which provides safety from attacks by aggressors. It means also economic security, social security, moral security—in a family of Nations.

Government has a sacred duty, in other words, to provide security as a fundamental human right.

Roosevelt was well aware that this was a departure from the traditional understanding of the role of American government:

> This Republic had its beginning, and grew to its present strength, under the protection of certain inalienable political rights—among them the right of free speech, free press, free worship, trial by jury, freedom from unreasonable searches and seizures. They were our rights to life and liberty. As our Nation has grown in size and stature, however—as our industrial economy expanded—these political rights proved inadequate to assure us equality in the pursuit of happiness. We have come to a clear realization of the fact that true individual freedom cannot exist without economic security and independence. "Necessitous men are not free men." People who are hungry and out of a job are the stuff of which dictatorships are made. In

our day these economic truths have become accepted as self-evident. We have accepted, so to speak, a second Bill of Rights under which a new basis of security and prosperity can be established for all....

Among these new rights, Roosevelt said, are:

> The right to a useful and remunerative job in the industries, or shops or farms or mines of the Nation; The right to earn enough to provide adequate food and clothing and recreation; The right of every farmer to raise and sell his products at a return which will give him and his family a decent living; The right of every businessman, large and small, to trade in an atmosphere of freedom from unfair competition and domination by monopolies at home or abroad; The right of every family to a decent home; The right to adequate medical care and the opportunity to achieve and enjoy good health; The right to adequate protection from the economic fears of old age, sickness, accident, and unemployment; The right to a good education.

The Constitution had established a limited government that presupposed an autonomous civil society and a free economy. But such freedom had led inevitably to social inequality, which in Roosevelt's view had made Americans insecure in a way that was unacceptable. He had lost faith in the older constitutional principle of limited government. Rather, he thought that the protection of political rights—or of social and economic liberty, exercised by individuals unregulated by government—had made it impossible to establish a foundation for social justice, that is, what he called "equality in the pursuit of happiness." He assumed that a fundamental tension exists between equality and liberty that can only be resolved by a powerful, even unlimited, administrative or welfare state.

Rejecting the Founders

The American founders, by contrast, thought that equality and liberty were perfectly compatible—indeed, that they were opposite sides of the same coin. The principle of natural equality had been set forth in the Declaration of Independence, which clearly spelled out the way in which all human beings are the same: They are equally endowed with natural and inalienable rights. But along with this similarity, the Founders knew that differences are sown into human nature: Some people are smarter, some are stronger, some are more beautiful, some are musically inclined while others have a predilection for business. Political equality, which requires the protection of individual rights, produces social inequality (or unequal achievement) precisely because of these unequal natural faculties.

The preservation of freedom, therefore, in the Founders' view, requires a defense of private property, understood in terms of the protection of the individual citizen's rights of conscience, opinion, self-interest, and labor. They thought that a constitutional order, by separating church and state, government and civil society, and the public and private sphere, makes it possible to reconcile equality and liberty in a reasonable way that is compatible with the nature of man. Thus the Constitution limits the power of government to the protection of natural rights.

Roosevelt and his fellow progressives rejected the idea of natural differences between men, insisting that those differences arise only out of social and economic inequality. As a result, they redefined the idea of freedom, divorcing it from the idea of individual rights and identifying it instead with the idea of security. It was in the cause of this new understanding of freedom that America's constitutional form of limited government was gradually replaced—beginning with the New Deal and culminating in the late 1960s and 1970s—by an administrative or welfare state.

Roosevelt had made it clear, even before he was elected president, that government had a new and different role to play in American life than that assigned to it by the Constitution. In an October 1932 radio address, he stated: "I have . . . described the spirit of my program as a 'new deal,' which is plain English for a changed concept of the duty and responsibility of Government toward economic life." In his view, selfish behavior on the part of individuals and corporations must give way to rational social action informed by a benevolent government and the organized intelligence of the bureaucracy. Consequently, the role of government was no longer the protection of the natural or political rights of individuals. The old constitutional distinction between government and society—or between the public and private spheres—as the ground of liberalism and a bulwark against political tyranny had created, in Roosevelt's view, economic tyranny. To solve this, government itself would become a tool of benevolence working on behalf of the people.

This redefinition of the role of government carried with it a new understanding of the role of the American people. In Roosevelt's Commonwealth Club address of 1932, he said:

> The Declaration of Independence discusses the problem of government in terms of a contract. . . . Under such a contract, rulers were accorded power, and the people consented to that power on consideration that they be accorded certain rights. The task of statesmanship has always been the redefinition of these rights in terms of a changing and growing social order. New conditions impose new requirements upon government and those who conduct government.

But this idea of a compact between government and the people is contrary to both the Declaration of Independence and the Constitution. Indeed, what links the Declaration and the Constitution is the idea of the people as autonomous and sovereign, and government as the people's creation and servant. Jefferson, in the Declaration, clearly presented the relationship in this way: "to secure these [inalienable] rights, governments are instituted among men, deriving their just powers from the consent of the governed. . . ."

Similarly, the Constitution begins by institutionalizing the authority of the people: "We the People of the United States, in Order to form a more perfect Union, establish Justice, insure domestic Tranquility, provide for the common defence, promote the general Welfare, and secure the Blessings of Liberty to ourselves and our Posterity, do ordain and establish this Constitution for the United States of America."

In Roosevelt's reinterpretation, on the other hand, government determines the conditions of social compact, thereby diminishing not only the authority of the Constitution but undermining the effective sovereignty of the people.

Reagan's Attempt to Turn the Tide

Ronald Reagan addressed this problem of sovereignty at some length in his First Inaugural, in which he observed famously: "In this present crisis, government is not the solution to our problem, government is the problem." He was speaking specifically of the deep economic ills that plagued the nation at the time of his election. But he was also speaking about the growing power of a bureaucratic and intellectual elite. This elite, he argued, was undermining the capacity of the people to control what had become, in effect, an unelected government. Thus it was undermining self-government itself.

The perceived failure of the U.S. economy during the Great Depression had provided the occasion for expanding the role of the federal government in administering the private sector. Reagan insisted in 1981 that government had proved itself incapable of solving the problems of the economy or of society. As for the relationship between the people and the government, Reagan did not view it, as Roosevelt had, in terms of the people consenting to the government on the condition that government grant them certain rights. Rather, he insisted:

> We are a nation that has a government—not the other way around. And this makes us special among the nations of the Earth. Our government has no power except that granted it by the people. It is time to check and reverse the growth of government, which shows signs of having grown beyond the consent of the governed.

In Reagan's view it was the individual, not government, who was to be credited with producing the things of greatest value in America:

> If we look to the answer as to why for so many years we achieved so much, prospered as no other people on Earth, it was because here in this land we unleashed the energy and individual genius of man to a greater extent than has ever been done before. Freedom and the dignity of the individual have been more available and assured here than in any other place on Earth.

And it was the lack of trust in the people that posed the greatest danger to freedom:

> [W]e've been tempted to believe that society has become too complex to be managed by self-rule, that government by an elite group is superior to government for, by, and of the people. Well, if no one among us is capable of governing himself, then who among us has the capacity to govern someone else?

Reagan had been long convinced that the continued growth of the bureaucratic state could lead to the loss of freedom. In his famous 1964 speech, "A Time for Choosing," delivered on behalf of Barry Goldwater, he had said:

> [I]t doesn't require expropriation or confiscation of private property or business to impose socialism on a people. What does it mean whether you hold the deed or the title to your business or property if the government holds the power of life and death over that business or property? Such machinery already exists. The government can find some charge to bring against any concern it chooses to prosecute. Every businessman has his own tale of harassment. Somewhere a perversion has taken place. Our natural, inalienable rights are now considered to be a dispensation of government, and freedom has never been so fragile, so close to slipping from our grasp as it is at this moment.

Reagan made it clear that centralized control of the economy and society by the federal government could not be accomplished without undermining individual rights and establishing coercive and despotic control.

> "[T]he full power of centralized government" was the very thing the Founding Fathers sought to minimize. They knew that governments don't control things. A government can't control the economy without controlling people. And they knew when a government sets out to do that, it must use force and coercion to achieve its purpose. They also knew,

those Founding Fathers, that outside of its legitimate functions, government does nothing as well or as economically as the private sector of the economy.

Over the next 15 years, Reagan succeeded in mobilizing a powerful sentiment against the excesses of big government. In doing so, he revived the debate over the importance of limited government for the preservation of a free society. This theme would remain constant throughout his presidency. In his final State of the Union message, Reagan proclaimed "that the most exciting revolution ever known to humankind began with three simple words: 'We the People,' the revolutionary notion that the people grant government its rights, and not the other way around." And in his Farewell Address to the nation, he said: "Ours was the first revolution in the history of mankind that truly reversed the course of government, and with three little words: 'We the People.'" He never wavered in his insistence that modern government had become a problem, primarily because it sought to replace the people as central to the American constitutional order.

Like the Founders, Reagan understood human nature to be unchanging—and thus tyranny, like selfishness, to be a problem coeval with human life. Experience had taught the Founders to regard those who govern with the same degree of suspicion as those who are governed—equally subject to selfish or tyrannical opinions, passions, and interests. Consequently, they did not attempt to mandate the good society or social justice by legislation, because they doubted that it was humanly possible to do so. Rather they attempted to create a free society, in which the people themselves could determine the conditions necessary for the good life. By establishing a constitutional government of limited power, they placed their trust in the people.

Up or Down, Not Right or Left

The political debate in America today is often portrayed as being between progressives (or the political left) and reactionaries (or the political right), the former working for change on behalf of a glorious future and the latter resisting that change. Reagan denied these labels because they are based on the idea that human nature can be transformed such that government can bring about a perfect society. In his 1964 speech, he noted:

> You and I are told increasingly that we have to choose between a left or right. Well I would like to suggest that there is no such thing as a left or right. There is only an up or down—up to man's age-old dream, the ultimate in individual freedom consistent with law and order, or down to the ant heap of totalitarianism. And regardless of their sincerity, their humanitarian motives, those who would trade our freedom for security have embarked on this downward course.

In light of the differences between the ideas and policies of Roosevelt and Reagan, it is not surprising that political debates today are so bitter. Indeed, they resemble the religious quarrels that once convulsed Western society. The progressive defenders of the bureaucratic state see government as the source of benevolence, the moral embodiment of the collective desire to bring about social justice as a practical reality. They believe that only mean-spirited reactionaries can object to a government whose purpose is to bring about this good end. Defenders of the older constitutionalism, meanwhile, see the bureaucratic state as increasingly tyrannical and destructive of inalienable rights.

Ironically, the American regime was the first to solve the problem of religion in politics. Religion, too, had sought to establish the just or good society—the city of God—upon earth. But as the Founders knew, this attempt had simply led to various forms of clerical tyranny. Under the American Constitution, individuals would have religious liberty but churches would not have the power to enforce their claims on behalf of the good life. Today, with the replacement of limited government constitutionalism by an administrative state, we see the emergence of a new form of elite, seeking to establish a new form of perfect justice. But as the Founders and Reagan understood, in the absence of angels governing men, or men becoming angels, limited government remains the most reasonable and just form of human government.

LARRY P. ARNN

A Return to the Constitution

It is a custom more honored in the breach than the observance.
—Hamlet, *Act I, Scene IV*

Even in *Hamlet,* where ghosts help the action along, it is necessary to choose between the breach and the observance of a custom. The Bard can twist things around plenty in his plays, but the law of contradiction is stubborn. For all his art, Shakespeare cannot make his characters do a thing and not do it at the same time.

We live in a more liberated age, the age of bureaucratic government. Here rules abound in such profusion that they seem to overbear the laws of nature themselves. So it is with honoring the Constitution these days. We honor it more avidly than ever in the breach of its restraints, but at the same time we pay it the respect of mandatory, hectic, and empty observance. Except for our dishonoring of it, we have never honored it so much.

Take two examples, the first from Senator Robert C. Byrd of West Virginia. He is the longest serving senator, and by reputation a great historian of that body and of the nation. He is fond of the Constitution of the United States. He talks of it often, and he carries a copy with him, he says, at all times. He is the author of a law now three years old that requires Constitution Day celebrations at schools and colleges across the land, if they take the federal dollar, which with rare exceptions they do. Never mind that there is a constitutional question about that federal dollar. We make it the ground of a federal command to respect the Constitution nonetheless. The government's breach is the authority for mandated observance.

In a fine quote, Senator Byrd calls upon us to make the Constitution an active part of our lives. He reminds us that we cannot defend and protect it if we are ignorant of its history and how it works. He recalls the "limits that the Constitution places on how political power is exercised," which limits have ensured our freedom for more than two centuries. Then he votes for earmarks on a scale to shame a Vermont liberal (or, these days, a Nebraska Republican), for subsidies to investigate the fluke and the flounder in maritime centers in landlocked states (especially his own, where the centers are named for him), and for every federal gazebo and portico from West Virginia to Baja. Whatever the "limits that the Constitution places on how political power is exercised," these days they leave the budget process in a position of latitude.

This is Senator Byrd, modern paragon of service to the Constitution.

The other example is from our most recent Constitution Day, September 17, 2007, the 220th anniversary of that greatest written instrument of government. I do not mean the official celebration, which was noble and good. The big Washington players of the day were not there, but Colin Powell read the Preamble aloud in the Capitol, and people around the world had a chance to read along by way of the Internet. Somehow Constitution Day manages to come off better than the other days that have grown up under the "national day of observance" laws that place Constitution Day on a par with National Maritime Day (May 22), America Recycles Day (November 15), and Pan American Day (April 14, which grants us a little gaiety before taxes come due).

Our second example is rather another ceremony happening on that day in Washington. Over in another part of town, in one of those newer sorts of buildings that now obscure and offend the lovely architecture of L'Enfant, a ceremony of a different sort was held. It was a ceremony of dedication to make a new hero out of an old name: Lyndon Baines Johnson. That name is now attached heroically to the building where the Department of Education resides. The family of President Johnson was present to receive honor for the mighty good he did for education.

The *Chronicle of Higher Education* did a good job covering this event. They put the main point first:

> Washington—A decade ago, Republicans were vying to eliminate the Education Department, deriding it as a wasteful expansion of federal authority. Today, they led a ceremony outside its headquarters here not only to celebrate the department, but to name the building after a trademark big-government Democrat from Texas: Lyndon Baines Johnson.

The first sentence recalls Republican platforms as recent as the one of 1996, which declares:

> Our formula is as simple as it is sweeping: the federal government has no constitutional authority to be involved in school curricula or to control jobs in the work place. That is why we will abolish the Department of Education, end federal meddling in our schools, and promote family choice at all levels of learning.

Reading this passage is like watching the first *Die Hard* movie, where Bruce Willis seems so young, and the movie for all its violence has a kind of innocence. That was before the real terror war. That was when we thought a man of action working under his own direction was the key to making great things happen. That was also when we thought that we could do something about the centralization of power that is the great tendency of the age. Having lost this innocence, now we are slightly embarrassed to read the naïveté of the 1996 Republican platform, or to think how foolish Ronald Reagan might have been to try to get rid of the Department of Education.

At the ceremony, Secretary of Education Margaret Spellings seems unaware of these former embarrassments, although we will shortly recite a little evidence that she is not. At the ceremony, she is full of the glories of the Great Society:

> Forty years ago, education was just beginning to transition from being a small office dedicated to gathering statistics. Today we're 4,500 strong, armed with computers and Blackberrys, and we're committed to a mission, ranging from financial aid to special education and to making sure that no child is left behind.

Note how the Secretary conflates the name of the office where she works with the thing that it regulates. The 4,500 people who work at the Department of Education are not teachers, at least not any more, and they do not directly accomplish education. But still, in some sense, they have become "education." It is they, and not the hundreds of thousands of teachers who work in education, nor the millions who have worked in it during the past 40 years, who make the difference in education. It is they, believes the Secretary, who leave no child behind. But that, alas, is a much easier thing to say than it is to do.

Never mind also, at least on this day, the 40 years of political history that have intervened since the Great Society. Never mind the service of President Reagan, whose political achievements provide the ground upon which Secretary Spellings stands, even if she is inclined to jump off it. In fact neither she nor President Bush would likely be in office but for him. This is such an obvious fact, and President Bush himself has so often spoken of the achievements of Reagan and his wish to emulate him, that it is hard to believe that Reagan now seems forgotten.

There is evidence that he is in fact not forgotten, but rather ignored. Secretary Spellings recently gave an interesting interview to *Human Events* reporter Terence Jeffrey. She was candid and intelligent in the interview, for one thing disarmingly ready to admit the failures of her policies so far, even while defending them and predicting their long-term success. She favors school choice and works to get it implemented, if so far without much success. She has tough words for the education union that is such a dreaded political obstacle to reform. But toward the end of the interview she was asked a pair of questions that she found difficult.

Mr. Jeffrey asked her if she could "point to language in the Constitution that authorized the federal government to have a Department of Education." Her reply shows that she knew the bearing of the inquiry: "I think we had come to an understanding, at least, of the reality of Washington and the flat world, if you will, that the Department of Education was not going to be abolished, and we were going to invest in our nation's neediest students."

Mr. Jeffrey persisted: "It is one thing to say that the political reality is we are not going to abolish the federal Department of Education, but can you seriously point to where the Framers actually intended the Constitution to authorize a Department of Education?"

The Secretary replied: "I can't point to it one way or the other. I'm not a constitutional scholar, but I'll look into it for you, Terry." Mr. Jeffrey reports that he did not get his answer.

This is Secretary of Education Margaret Spellings, sworn to uphold the Constitution in the exercise of her office.

Secretary Spellings and her department provide an example to stand for the rest of the federal domestic establishment. It is the archetype of our current condition and the direction in which we travel. It is doing what the rest are doing, and it is doing it for the same reasons. In examining it, we can see both the problem and the solution.

The Department of Education grows now at a rate much faster than the Department of Defense, even in time of war. It grows much faster than the domestic economy, even now when the economy grows rapidly. It grows faster than the population it serves, even when that population is growing. The pace of its growth will quicken with the recent passage of the Higher Education Access Act of 2007, which reduces the size of student loan subsidies, but redeploys that money into outright grants, loan forgiveness, and new programs. If the past is prologue, these new programs will grow as fast as the old ones have done.

Why would this be happening in a Republican administration, the first in a generation (prior to the 2006 elections) to control both houses of Congress along with the White House? The people involved are not for the most part corrupt or ill-intended; surely Secretary Spellings is neither. Something strong is moving them and her. There are two kinds of things.

The first kind is found in the obstacles anyone in office must face. Education is desperately in need of reform; for example, our high school graduates have math and science scores at the bottom of the industrialized world. The longer they are in school, the lower they fall. When one attempts to repair this, one meets quickly the most powerful of public sector lobbies, the education union. Its members have a vested interest to protect and the prestige that comes rightly from serving, but not rightly when only seeming to serve, the young. Finally, the cost and complication of college is fearsome to parents, who are unaware that the subsidies and outside interests that control education make both of them worse. It is very difficult in the circumstances to do anything good.

The second kind is to be found inside the Secretary and other parts of the Administration. They are drawn to the principles of the Great Society. In her interview with Terence Jeffrey, Secretary Spellings refers to the "flat world." Doubtless she means the pressure of globalized economic competition made possible by global communications. She likes to say in her speeches that, to face this competition, we have to emulate the achievement of the Great Society. She mentions in particular the response to the Sputnik crisis, which was a great national effort to subsidize higher education and thereby beat the Soviet Union to the moon. Now we can beat China and other competitors economically by the same device.

From a simple chronological point of view, the example of the Sputnik crisis does not quite work. There was not enough time for the federal programs to educate any appreciable number of scientists to participate in the NASA programs that got us to the moon. Twelve years elapsed between the Sputnik and the landing on the moon; one does not produce astrophysicists very quickly. The mistake goes deeper than a point of chronology. It involves a mistake about the nature of constitutional government and the source of American power. And this is connected to a mistake about the purpose of education itself.

These two mistakes are closely related. The American government is explicitly, and to a unique degree, justified by an account of the nature of man and his relation to God above and the beasts below. This involves a perception, not of utility here on earth, but rather of the order of nature against which all utility must be judged. In the old understanding of America, the one propagated by those who made the nation, the preparation for leadership and for excellent living consisted in the contemplation of this order and the study of its application to our lives.

One cannot miss this if he studies old documents, both about the making of the Constitution and about the founding of colleges. Our own college, by no means unique in this respect, was built in service of the blessings of "civil and religious liberty and intelligent piety." The first two are civic goods, achieved first in the American Republic. To secure these blessings, we promise an education that will "develop the minds and improve the hearts" of our students. In other words, the purpose of education has both an intellectual and a moral component, and these are connected essentially. One will find these sentiments in the founding of nearly any old college of quality.

One will find them also in the founding documents of the country. They are present most famously in the Northwest Ordinance, which in its third article proclaims that "Religion, morality, and knowledge, being necessary to good government and the happiness of mankind, schools and the means of education shall forever be encouraged." In other words, good living both in the private and the public sense requires knowledge of the things above. The purpose of education, and especially of higher education, is to come to know and contemplate these higher things.

One will not find these sentiments in the plans for education made in the Department of Education today. Of course it would be difficult to put them there: Religion, for one thing, has now been systematically excluded from the public schools as a matter, purportedly, of constitutional law. There is, however, no sign that the people in charge of the department have any wish to include them. The report of the National Commission on the Future of Higher Education reduces education to the purpose of preparing young people for a job and of making the nation powerful and successful in its economic competition with other nations. The idea—questionable upon its face—is that only a national coordinated effort can make us formidable to China, for example. China is indeed growing rapidly. This has become possible only because, under duress and against its every wish, the government of China has liberated its people to start their own businesses and make their own plans. They seek to emulate our successes to the extent that they are forced. We seek to emulate their failures because we find them attractive.

What then is to be done?

In this gloomy picture there is no major national force, at least no political force, united to support constitutional government in its old and proven sense. If we cannot find our solution in the present, then we must look to the past. One of those successes is the recently rejected example of Ronald Reagan. When Reagan began his career it seemed simply impossible to resist this type of bureaucratic government, just as it seems today. He proceeded nonetheless, in part because he had a clear understanding of the purpose both of education and of constitutional government. About the purpose of education, he said:

> "Train up the child in the way he should go," Solomon wrote, "and when he's old he will not depart from it." That is the God-given responsibility of each parent, the compact with each teacher, and the trust of every child.

In another place he revels in the love of the founders for education and their faith "that an educated populace would guarantee the success of this great experiment in democracy. . . ."

As for the organization of education, Reagan understood it from the constitutional perspective of self-government. His First Inaugural, a worthy successor to the greatest inaugural speeches of the greatest presidents, is built around the theme of self-government and the association of every American with the great heroes of America, including Washington, Lincoln, and Jefferson, in the practice and defense of self-government. In another speech he said:

> Our leaders must remember that education doesn't begin with some isolated bureaucrat in Washington. It doesn't even begin with State or local officials. Education begins in the home, where it's a parental right and responsibility. Both our public and our private schools exist to aid our families in the instruction of our children, and it's time some people back in Washington stopped acting as if family wishes were only getting in the way.

A government that forgets this sentiment is not competent to give instructions for higher education. Forgetting the purpose of education, such a government is likely to forget its own purpose, too. That is dangerous both to liberty and to justice.

The question of what is to be done is simple to answer: It is not enough anymore to rehearse by rote the Constitution or to celebrate it in vacuous observances. Both our statesmen and our citizens must return first to its study, with depth and intensity, and then to its sustenance, with eloquence and resolve. Nothing else will do.

DOUG BANDOW

The History and Track Record
of Social Security

Historical Heritage

The welfare state was essentially born in Otto von Bismarck's Germany. The famed Iron Chancellor was concerned about the electoral appeal of the social democrats, and hit upon the idea of making the citizens dependent on the state. Germany's Social Security system was created in 1889; it eventually spread, in many guises, to many nations.

Germany's program still exists. However, the country's tax rate is set to rise from 19.5 percent today to 22 percent by 2030. Benefits are declining and the retirement age is rising. Economic reality is hitting the birthplace of the welfare state.

Because of America's more individualistic philosophical heritage, and the lack of a serious socialist party, it wasn't until the Great Depression that many politicians began to believe it necessary to provide social benefits to save our political system.

In the U.S., Social Security was approved in 1935, an early victory for Franklin Delano Roosevelt as he rapidly expanded government control over the economy in an attempt to reverse the Depression. People's needs were great and the pressures on government to act were strong. Today we know more about that tragic time: Mismanagement of the money supply and misguided protectionism were the most important factors in triggering the economic collapse, while attempts to cartelize the economy under both Herbert Hoover and FDR did much to prolong the downturn.

Back then people didn't understand why the economy had collapsed, and they were desperate for most any action. Roosevelt was an experimenter more interested in acting than in worrying about what his actions would accomplish. Even now he is celebrated for restoring American confidence, an odd compliment for someone who recklessly embraced so many counterproductive initiatives. Many of them, such as the National Recovery Act, sharply worsened America's economic plight.

For Roosevelt Social Security's most important benefit, however, was political: He recognized that once Americans were hooked on government benefits, they were likely to vote for more programs. In his view it was important to create individual accounts—fiction, but effective nonetheless—to make people believe they had a stake in the program and so prevent its repeal by a future Republican Congress.

Conservative legislators fought the bill, but early in the New Deal Roosevelt's authority was great—and the Democratic Party's congressional margin even greater. The Social Security program began in 1937 for workers; spousal and survivor benefits were added in 1939; disability benefits were added later.

Although Social Security has long been viewed as the "third rail" of American politics—touch it and die—it is better seen as a symbol of America's entitlement culture. Although the U.S. lags behind Europe, it nevertheless has constructed an expansive and expensive welfare state. Social Security and Medicare are the foundation, to which Medicaid, health care for the poor, was added in 1964. There are federal, state, and local pensions, which have become budget-busters. There is unemployment insurance. There are jobs programs and training programs, endless "economic development" subsidies, grants and loans for businesses, loans for students, and much, much more.

It should come as no surprise, then, that the budget results have been ugly and the future looks even worse. Current projections suggest that federal spending as a percentage of GDP will rise from 20 percent today to 34 percent by 2030. That is higher than at any other point since World War II. Toss in state and local spending and half the economy will be in government hands. These estimates ignore the natural tendency of government outlays to climb far faster and further than projected.

Although virtually all spending programs seem to continue to go up, regardless of results, these outlandish increases are concentrated in the big three: Social Security, Medicare, and Medicaid. Pork barrel waste, special interest earmarks, and corporate welfare might get the most public attention, but Uncle Sam's credit is at risk because of income transfers through retirement and medical programs.

These daunting numbers did not stop the Republican president and Republican Congress from creating yet another entitlement program, the Medicare drug benefit—the biggest expansion of the welfare state in 40 years. Supporters cheered because competition among private insurers has held premium costs below predictions, but that will only slightly lower the height of the financial tsunami as roughly 77 million baby boomers begin to retire in 2008. Providing third-party "insurance" coverage for drugs has the same effect on the demand for pharmaceuticals as it has had on other medical services.

Indeed, over the next 75 years the pharmaceutical program is predicted to run to more than $8 trillion, nearly one-third of Medicare's current unfunded liabilities and more than Social Security's deficit. And that is assuming there are no changes, which is unlikely once recipients discover that Congress has created a so-called "doughnut-hole" through which coverage disappears at mid-expenditure levels.

Over the long term Social Security and Medicare are the true budget busters: In 2005 they accounted for $518 billion and $290 billion in outlays, respectively. Together they account for almost one-third of federal spending. Medicaid ran about $192 billion in the same year. The three hit about 40 percent of the budget. If the federal budget stays the same as a share of national income, by 2030 these three programs will consume 75 percent of the budget. This doesn't leave much for the military, interest, poverty programs, or anything else.

Although Social Security currently outspends Medicare, the latter is the bigger long-term problem. Its financial outlook is "much worse than Social Security's," declared the Social Security and Medicare trustees two years ago. By 2024 Medicare outlays are expected to exceed those for Social Security; left unchanged, Medicare will spend twice as much as Social Security by 2078. Douglas Holtz-Eakin, director of the Congressional Budget Office, warns that the growth in Medicare is "simply unsustainable."

Even these estimates understate likely outlays. Michael Cannon of the Cato Institute notes "there is constant pressure to expand Medicare benefits—from seniors, health care interest groups, and advocates of socialized medicine. Recent examples include the new prescription drug benefit, as well as coverage for preventive screening, obesity, and quit-smoking programs that President Bush added by fiat."

Social Security and Medicare are disastrously unbalanced for three reasons. First, "contributions" to Social Security and Medicare are insufficient to provide promised benefits. Both programs are primarily funded by taxes on the rest of the population.

Second, demographics: Quite simply, life expectancy is up and fertility rates are down. The population is aging as the number of elderly explodes, and the elderly are living longer.

Third, and unique to health care, is the continuing rapid increase in health care outlays. Over the last 35 years Medicare outlays have risen 3 percent annually above the increase in per capita GDP. Since the elderly consume far more medical care than younger Americans, health-care cost inflation compounds the underlying demographic changes.

Worst is tomorrow's bill. Writes Chris Edwards of the Cato Institute: "In addition to today's federal public debt of $3.9 trillion, taxpayers may be on the hook for $2.9 trillion in federal employee retirement benefits, $1 trillion in veterans' benefits, $3.6 trillion in Social Security benefits, $15.6 trillion in Medicare benefits, and $7 trillion in the new Medicare drug benefits." But Edwards' figures merely run for 75 years. (Forget claims about accumulated assets in the Social Security and health insurance "trust funds," which are accounting fictions filled with special, nonmarketable treasury bonds.)

The 2005 annual report of the Board of Trustees of Social Security and Medicare states: "Even a 75-year period is not long enough to provide a complete picture of Social Security's financial condition." Jagadeesh Gokhale, now of the Cato Institute and then of the American Enterprise Institute, and Kent Smetters, a professor at the University of Pennsylvania, propose a measure of "fiscal imbalance" (FI) with an infinite time horizon. Their 2003 FI estimate was $44.2 trillion. Social Security ran $7 trillion and Medicare accounted for $36.6 trillion. The rest of the federal government ran just $0.5 trillion.

The FI worsens over time. It "grows by about $1.6 trillion per year to about $54 trillion by just 2008 unless corrective policies are implemented before then," say Gohkale and Smetters. Long-term estimates obviously are sensitive to economic assumptions: The FI could run to "only" $29 trillion if we are lucky or $64 trillion if things go less well.

The government's estimates, based on more pessimistic economic assumptions, are even more forbidding. Two years ago the Social Security and Medicare trustees estimate the full unfunded liability for Social Security to be $11.1 trillion. Medicare's unfunded hospital and medical insurance liability runs a shocking $49.9 trillion. And the new drug benefit, which had not been passed when Gokhale and Smetter completed their analysis, adds another $18.2 trillion. The total: $79.2 trillion.

By way of comparison, the federal government spends about $2.7 trillion a year, the entire public debt is $4.6 trillion, America's annual GDP is about $12 trillion, and Americans' total personal financial net worth is around $35 trillion.

The Congressional Budget Office figures that under intermediate program assumptions, federal outlays on Social Security, Medicare, and Medicaid will climb from 9 percent of GDP in 2010 to 17.7 percent in 2050. The more realistic "pessimistic" assumptions generate respective forecasts of 9.5 percent and 27.6 percent, or more than one of every four dollars generated by the entire economy. That doesn't include spending on the military, all other federal activities, and states and localities.

Comptroller General David M. Walker has warned: "The only thing the United States is able to do a little after 2040 is pay interest on massive and growing federal debt. The model blows up in the mid-2040s. What does that mean? Argentina."

We must confront the welfare state, and the entitlement mentality that underlies it. To do that, we must confront Social Security. (So too must we deal with Medicare and Medicaid, but the afflictions of the health care system are even more complex than those facing the retirement system. Thus, the topic must be left for a future essay.)

Indeed, Social Security may have become the third rail in both directions. Touch it and you die politically. Don't touch it and you die economically.

Of course, even today Social Security has its defenders. The Social Security Administration regularly extols the diverse benefits provided, the number of elderly lifted from poverty, the security of a government system, the way in which the program brings the middle class and poor together, the political advantages of a system that delivers benefits to the middle class, and so on. Carroll Estes, president of the Gerontological Society of America, contends: "Social Security is the most successful antipoverty program we have. When you have a program that works, why try to fix it?" Why indeed?

There is the little problem of the coming financial tsunami, and the possible battle among generations. More people under the age of 35 believe in UFOs than expect Social Security to pay them retirement benefits. That belief is not groundless. The only way current retirees will receive their benefits is for current workers to pay far higher taxes. The only way to reduce burgeoning costs is to cut benefits. The combination of higher taxes and lower benefits is an awful return.

Nonetheless, the program has seemed to work for most of its history. What has gone wrong and how can we fix it?

When Congress created Social Security seven decades ago, it worked for the same reason any Ponzi scheme seems to "work" at the beginning. A lot more people were paying into Social Security than were being paid by Social Security. For years, a few retirees were supported by many workers who paid low taxes—$60 maximum a year in 1937. The payroll tax started out at 2 percent on employers and employees combined. Congress cheerfully predicted that outlays in 1980 would run $3.5 billion.

The result was a secure system that delivered a high financial return, several times the total employer/employee contributions. The very first recipient, Miss Ida May Fuller, paid (both herself and through her employer) just $49.50 in taxes before she retired. She lived to be 100, and collected $22,888.92 in benefits. Although not all early recipients made out so well, many received back their life-time "contribution" in months rather than years. It seemed like a good deal for all. Legislators, in turn, reaped enormous political benefit.

The system continued to "work"—charging relatively low tax rates while providing steadily increasing benefits to an ever-growing

number of people—into the early 1980s. For this reason the program earned a reputation as the vanquisher of elder poverty. Over
time Republicans became almost as steadfast in their support of the
program as were Democrats. Unfortunately, all good things must
come to an end.

When Social Security began, many people died before collecting
a single check. In 1940, for instance, only 54 percent of men and 61
percent of women lived to the age of 65. Indeed, over six decades,
life expectancy has risen by 12 years, from 63 to 75. It is expected to
hit 80 by 2050. At the same time, the birth rate has fallen. Fertility
levels have dropped from 3.56 in 1900 to barely 2, below replacement level.

Together these two trends have had dramatic effect. There were
42 workers for every Social Security beneficiary in 1940 and 16 in 1950.
That ratio is now about 3.4 to 1. Thus, rather than spending $3.5 billion
on Social Security in 1980, Uncle Sam spent $105 billion, 30 times as
much. That number has increased more than fivefold since.

The numbers will continue to worsen. Between 2000 and 2045
the number of 65-year-olds and older will more than double, increasing at over five times the rate of 20- to 64-year-olds. Depending on the
rate of immigration, seniors may make up one-third of the population.
By the year 2025 the worker-beneficiary ratio will be barely two to
one, and it will fall slowly from there. Alex Pollock of the American
Enterprise Institute figures that a ratio of two-to-one requires annual
savings of 14 percent of pretax income, a huge hit on most families.

Even this may understate the problem. Economist Jenny
Roback points out that fertility rates have fallen well below replacement levels for middle-to-higher income Americans. Those are the
people whose children can be expected to contribute most financially
to Social Security. Further, shrinking family size means more than
just fewer workers to support each retiree. Declining fertility rates
also mean there will be fewer family members to provide informal,
nongovernment assistance.

As the demographics change, so has the economics. Since 1950
Congress has increased taxes about five times as much as benefits.
The 2 percent (on the first $3,000 earned!) reached 6 percent by
1960 and 12.4 percent (on $97,500 now earned) today. The 1983

"compromise" bail-out increased taxes, cut benefits, and raised the retirement age, reducing the rate of return on everyone's Social Security "investment." Four in five workers now pay more in payroll levies than in income taxes.

As taxes have risen, returns to retirees have plunged. In 1995 the first Americans retired who will lose money on their Social Security investment. The class was small: high income men who never married. But, increasingly, future retirees are looking at mere parity and, over time, growing losses. With rising taxes and falling benefits, the good deals received by the first beneficiaries are long gone.

The current average rate of return for recipients is just 2 percent, and under 1.5 percent for most workers. Most new workers will lose money. In contrast, the average annual return on stocks is 7.56 percent. The worst 20-year period in American history, an anomaly that included the Great Depression, 1929 to 1948, saw an annual rate of return of 3.36 percent. The Cato Institute figures that the average low-wage worker will receive $8,500 annually from Social Security, compared to $17,000 from comparable private accounts. The figures for an average wage worker are $15,200 and $39,000. For a high wage worker the numbers are $22,600 and $94,000. In short, everyone benefits from a freer, private retirement system.

Ironically, for a system presented as helping lower income people and the disadvantaged, the system works against the interests of women and many minorities. The rules, developed for two-parent, single-earner households, discriminate against single workers, dual-earner couples, and early divorcees. Groups with shorter life expectancies, such as African-Americans, receive less back in benefits. Although poor people receive a boost—the benefit calculation is modestly progressive—they also tend to live shorter lives than do their wealthier neighbors. Moreover, Social Security benefits alone are unlikely to keep them out of poverty.

But the ultimate symbol of the Social Security's problem is the fact that by 2017, within a decade, the system's outflow will exceed its income. Of course, system apologists argue that the trust fund surplus will carry forward another couple of decades (2040 is the current estimate). But there is no trust fund, at least as we normally understand it. Social Security is a pay-as-you-go program under which current revenues are used to pay current beneficiaries. Today there is a "surplus," but it is lent to the federal government to help cover the deficit. The trust fund actually consists of a pile of federal IOUs in a file cabinet in a government office in West Virginia. True, the Treasury Department promises to repay the loans, but to do so will require either tax hikes or spending cuts—the same as though there were no "trust fund." In short, the crisis comes sooner, not later.

It is a sobering analysis. But the problem is not just fiscal: It is cultural. Entitlement programs, as well as their means of financing, have adverse consequences. Most obviously, government pensions naturally encourage earlier retirement. A study by the National Center for Policy Analysis notes that the percentage of men over 65 who work has dropped in half to about 20 percent. (The percentage of women has stayed roughly constant.) Work participation fell both as a larger percentage of men were covered by Social Security, and benefits rose to a larger share of their previous incomes. This, of course, increases the public burden.

A government retirement income also discourages private saving in two ways. It takes money that otherwise would be invested; it also makes private saving less necessary.

Moreover, payroll taxes act as a direct levy on employment, discouraging job creation.Perhaps most insidiously, just as Otto von Bismarck expected, these programs also make Americans ever more dependent on government.

The latter is not something that is much discussed in Washington, DC, of course. There federal money is presumed to be owned by no one, but instead is a great common pool to be handed out by the government. But the money obviously isn't free: It doesn't come from some grateful Mideast sheik, for instance. It involves redistribution in two different forms.

First, Social Security takes money from workers and gives it to retirees. The latter have no special moral claim, other than having been taxed to support previous beneficiaries, to their checks; rather, the program simply takes from some for the benefit of others.

Second, Social Security redistributes responsibility for caring for the elderly from individuals and families to the state. Along the way, by having taxed away money that could otherwise have been invested in private retirement assets, the government has reduced private savings and pensions. In short, government takes money from people as they are working, and then after they are retired.

Moreover, shifting responsibility for the care of the elderly has important consequences. There is no doubt that caring for different generations within a family can be difficult and even unpleasant. But intergenerational ties are among the most important sinews of community. Social Security weakens these links, and makes it hard for a family to offer better care for its more vulnerable members. Denying younger workers the ability to achieve a higher return throughout their working lives leaves them with less money to share with their parents and older relatives.

It is no surprise that the longer we wait, the more difficult it becomes to close the gap. Indeed, the cost of waiting is about $800 billion a year—if measured by the size of the growing overall deficit. Since reforms are hardest to apply to those who have already retired, "Delaying action until the baby boom is in full retirement insures that the next generation will bear the burden of current inaction," argue Andrew J. Rettenmaier and Thomas R. Saving, for the Private Enterprise Research Center at Texas A&M University.

There are three general alternatives. The first is to tinker, while keeping Social Security essentially as it is. The second is to privatize the system by paying off current retirees and mandating private retirement contributions. The third is to abolish Social Security.

Tinkering with the *Titanic*

Most establishment defenders of Social Security advocate some combination of higher taxes and lower benefits. But making the numbers work isn't easy.

For instance, to save the system through tax hikes alone would require a 50 percent increase in Social Security levies by 2030. Adding in Medicare, to continue paying promised benefits would require all of currently collected payroll taxes plus 90 percent of existing income taxes. Similarly, to solve the problem through benefit cuts would require slashing promised payments. Both approaches would make

Social Security an even worse "deal" for recipients. Neither approach seems likely in today's political climate.

Again, it is worth considering Social Security in the larger context of runaway entitlement spending. Gokhale and Smetters estimate a total of $64 trillion in unfunded liabilities. How to eliminate them? Double the corporate and personal income taxes. Cut Medicare and Social Security by two-thirds. Eliminate all federal discretionary spending (for instance, maintaining the Washington Monument)—and even that only comes close.

A mix might be more realistic. One could raise the retirement age (currently set to increase to 67 in the year 2027), adjust the consumer price index (which some economists argue overstates the cost of living by 0.5 to 1.5 percent a year), abolish early retirement (now available at age 62), and reduce benefits (cap the cost of living adjustment, for instance). Alternatively (or simultaneously), one could hike taxes, either raising the FICA levy or increasing income taxes on Social Security benefits (currently half of payments are subject to the income tax). Or personal and corporate income taxes could be hiked with the money raised credited against Social Security.

Other possibilities include bringing state and municipal workers into the system and means testing benefits, that is, reducing or eliminating checks to wealthier retirees. More recent proposals would allow the government to invest some tax payments in the stock market.

Almost all Social Security defenders want to take some combination of these steps. The chief argument for doing so is that it would allow the system to stagger along for some period of time. The downside is rather serious, however: Most of these "reforms" reduce the return received by retirees while only postponing the crisis. At the same time, some of them would be as politically difficult to enact as more comprehensive reform. If the government is prepared to enact sharp tax hikes or means test benefits, then why not go the next step and seek a truly permanent solution?

Moreover, none of the suggested half-steps address the moral issues: the problems of shifting responsibility for the elderly to the government and increased dependence on government. As long as these are not addressed, the system will remain fundamentally flawed.

Privatizing the Bankrupt Concern

A more serious option is to privatize Social Security. Proposals for doing so abound. The Cato Institute has offered one of the most comprehensive plans, though groups like the National Center for Policy Analysis and the Heritage Foundation have developed similar initiatives. The basic approach is simple: Allow workers to opt out of Social Security through contributions to IRAs.

The best model in practice is Chile. In 1981 that nation inaugurated a private system. Starting in 1982, new workers contributed to one of 21 approved private pension funds rather than to the state system. Current workers were allowed to choose, and upward of 95 percent voluntarily shifted to private investments. The experience has proved to be an extraordinarily good deal for the people of Chile. The average compound annual rate of return was far higher than anything under the government plan, and the economy, flush with investment funds, has grown steadily.

The advantages of taking such an approach in America are obvious: People would regain control over their own retirement and earn a much higher rate of return on their contributions. They would be investing in real retirement programs, rather than dumping their money into a public scheme that would be illegal were it privately run. And they would own their assets, which would guarantee their benefits against political changes and allow them to be passed on to their heirs should they die prematurely.

Nevertheless, this sort of privatization has two major problems. The first is the short-term cost. If workers redirect their taxes while the government continues to pay current beneficiaries, the transition will be costly. Unless this sort of reform is coupled with means-testing, for example, it would require either higher taxes or large spending cuts elsewhere in the budget, neither of which typically appeal to the legislators who would have to approve such a program.

The second downside is that such a system continues to preserve an important role for government in Americans' retirement. Washington would still mandate savings, regulate plans, and otherwise intrude.

Nevertheless, privatization would be a major leap forward.

Abolishing the Failed Ponzi Scheme

The simplest solution is abolition. Social Security could simply be repealed. Young workers below a certain age, probably in their 40s, depending upon income level, would benefit from an immediate shift to a private retirement system. They would have no complaint, since they can invest what would have been future taxes and receive a better return. Although the specific results would vary by age, most would be better off.

Older workers over the break point could still invest, but would lose on net. Since they would earn the higher returns from a private system for at least some period of time, however, they would be able to moderate their loss. Retirees, those currently relying on Social Security benefits, would lose the most (though some would actually have received far more than they and their employers had contributed), and would have the greatest cause for complaint since they had relied on the government to their detriment.

The answer—should any president and Congress be so bold, or foolhardy, to adopt this course—would be for the federal government to undertake a massive asset sale. A half-billion acres of forest and range land, massive business enterprises such as the Postal Service and Power Marketing Administrations, office buildings both in the U.S. and abroad (unnecessary embassies and consulates, in particular), military equipment (made redundant through downsizing), and more could be placed on the market. In addition, government should privatize services and sell off the relevant agencies' facilities. A serious sale could generate hundreds of billions, probably trillions, of dollars.

This money could be used to purchase annuities for needy retirees and those approaching retirement. The money might not be enough for a full retirement package, but it should be considered merely one part of a comprehensive solution involving aid from families and charities as well.

Practical Reform Course

Of these three alternatives, the third is the most consistent and principled, but probably would get no votes other than that of Representative Ron Paul (R-TX). The first is the worst idea, preserving the system's many flaws while exacerbating the future costs for the rest of us. Thus, the second almost certainly is the best, most realistic approach.

Of course, a wide variety of possible specific plans are available. All would offer a significant improvement over the existing system; the political zeitgeist would determine which might be the most likely to win approval.

1. Several principles should guide reform efforts. First, any entitlements provided should create the least taxpayer burden. As noted earlier, entitlements are already driving federal spending upward. Social Security and related programs should not be given a blank check. If Social Security outlays can't be curbed politically, then other expenditures should be cut to accommodate entitlement growth.

Given current tax rates and rates of return, the starting point for any reform should be no tax hike. Perhaps the favorite idea is raising or lifting the earnings cap, which would impose a huge tax hike on the upper-middle class. The disproportionate tax hit would run in the thousands of dollars and would fall hardest on those whose return from Social Security already is anemic. A tax hike of this magnitude — about $1.4 trillion over 10 years — also would notably discourage job creation. The Heritage Foundation figures this could destroy a million jobs.

No surprise, then, that House Ways and Means Committee Chairman Charlie Rangel (D-NY) proclaims himself ready to hike levies, and the White House has given some evidence of its willingness to go along as part of a comprehensive package. Nervous conservatives are circulating news accounts of the first President Bush, who publicly rejected proposals for a tax hike before signing onto a revenue-raising package that contributed to his electoral defeat. Yet many Democrats insist on negotiations that exclude any possibility of individual accounts, which means negotiations to surrender. Any such approach would simply be rearranging the deck chairs on the *Titanic*, using some mix of tax hikes and benefit cuts, thereby making Social Security an even worse deal for America's workers.

Moreover, dramatically hiking taxes on professionals and small businessmen—a 12.4 percent marginal jump—likely would encourage them to work less and save less, as well as retire earlier, thereby collecting even more benefits. Larry Lindsey, former chief White House economic adviser, figures that this group is particularly sensitive to marginal tax hikes. Behavioral changes in response to the increase levy would offset about 70 percent of the presumed revenue increase, dropping the annual take from $82 billion (in 2004) to just $27 billion. Fully lifting the earnings cap would delay Social Security's insolvency by only six years—to 2023. Adjusted for Lindsey's estimates, the impact would be far less. At some point such a policy risks becoming self-defeating.

2. Benefits must be addressed since demographic changes have made current payments unsustainable. The problem, however, is figuring out how to achieve both generational and practical equity. Gokhale and Smetters note that "past and living generations are projected to receive $8.8 trillion more in benefits than they will contribute in payroll taxes," but "future generations are projected to pay $1.7 trillion more in taxes than they will receive in benefits."

Taxing future generations even more to pay for current benefits would exacerbate the unfairness. But Gokhale and Smetters figure that meeting the shortfall solely through benefit cuts would require reductions approaching 60 percent. Political considerations dictate some degree of protection for current beneficiaries, lest the perfect, unattainable reform become the enemy of good, achievable one.

Current beneficiaries rely on the program, so it would be best if they had time to adapt to the changes. That suggests largely guaranteeing the benefits for current recipients while concentrating changes for younger workers well before they retire. One such proposal, from Wall Street Democrat Robert Pozen, is "progressive indexing," which would raise Social Security benefits by the cost-of-living index rather than cost-of-wages index, which artificially inflates benefits. (Under current law, real Social Security payments are expected to double by 2077; the Pozen plan, depending on how it was implemented, would reduce real benefits by about one-third.)

3. Washington must beware making the problem worse through seemingly ancillary policy changes. For instance, the U.S. apparently has reached a so-called totalization agreement with Mexico, which sorts out retirement benefits for expatriates of both nations who are living in the other. Critics worry that the pact might enable any illegal aliens who benefited from a future amnesty to collect benefits for work performed while in America illegally. Government spokesman have denied that the agreement includes any such provision, but no one knows what a immigration reform bill might include.

Totalization agreements, mostly made with smaller European states, usually are neither expensive nor controversial. But the question of Mexican immigration raises unique challenges. Whatever one thinks about that issue, the government should not add to Social Security's fiscal burdens without careful thought.

4. The most effective measures should prolong worklife and delay retirement. More work reduces the need for government income support, while later retirement reduces program expenditures. Longer life expectancies make this principle a matter of justice as well as practicality. When Social Security was created many people died before collecting their first check. Now most not only collect their first check, but collect for years — a wonderful testament to modern technology, but a bane for the federal budget. Government could increase the retirement age and the financial penalty for early retirement. Reducing taxes for those who continue to work after they have become eligible for Social Security is another possible step.

5. People need to save more for many purposes, from retirement to health care. In particular, government needs to increase incentives for private retirement assets. Over the last two decades private retirement accounts have jumped from $1.5 trillion to $6.5 trillion. Creating private Social Security accounts is the most obvious step to take.

Full privatization would be even better. Allowing people to voluntarily opt out of Social Security and put the equivalent of their Social Security taxes into private accounts would ultimately reduce program outlays. Public contributions to private accounts, or even continuation of the existing program, could be limited to those of the least means. Martin Feldstein figures that even partial substitution of private retirement accounts "would eliminate the need for a future increase in the Social Security payroll tax."

Roughly 30 nations have such programs. All vary to some degree and none have been trouble-free, but most have delivered a more remunerative, more secure retirement future for their people. The Chilean model, for instance, has been widely copied, spreading to Argentina, Mexico, and Uruguay, as well as Hungary and other nations. Basically, workers own their accounts and choose their own fund managers.

Another version, termed the OECD model, has been adopted by nations as different as Australia, Britain, and Switzerland. Generally there is some form of group plan, where a business or union chooses an investment plan for everyone. Some have allowed greater individual choice as well.

A few countries, such as Sweden, have sought to avoid the costs of making a transition by creating notional individual accounts. That is, the system is still pay-as-you-go, with defined contributions rather than benefits, but people receive the illusion of having separate accounts. Sweden has added a small funded component that workers can choose their investments.

Expanded IRAs are another option, should Social Security reform prove impossible.

Overall, many nations are undergoing even greater demographic challenges than America, resulting in even worse economic problems. Governments have responded in many ways, ranging from privatization to cost-cutting. Reporting on Europe, analyst Gary Burtless says, "With respect to pension policy, national governments have increased contribution rates to the public programs, overhauled pension schedules to reduce promised future benefits, and introduced new features in public pension and old-age unemployment programs to encourage employment after the early or standard retirement age."

6. The U.S. needs to address the welfare state more comprehensively. We need to reshape entitlement programs to allow people to opt out, while shifting benefits from higher- to lower-income retirees. The moral imperative is to care for those least able to care for themselves. Ultimately, full means testing would help cut costs and establish self-reliance as the operating principle for all but the indigent.

The politics of such an approach is not easy, though Canada and Great Britain have incorporated means testing in their policies. Another possibility would be to end benefits for those at the highest income levels. Or, as proposed by President George W. Bush, one could begin to slow cost-of-living increases for higher income Social Security recipients.

Although such steps may not seem "fair," existing beneficiaries are receiving far more than they paid into the system. Those who can best afford to bear the sort of benefit reductions necessary to hold down overall program costs are those who least need the benefits. This approach would move "social insurance" toward simple welfare.

7. Other government expenditures need to be cut sharply. Unfortunately, there is no way around "transition costs" of any reform—essentially the price of simultaneously allowing people to shift their (forced) contributions to private accounts while paying currently promised benefits. Taxpayer money should not be wasted at any time, but especially now. Every low priority should be targeted, and the stark choice posed: Do you want to take care of seniors or [fill in the blank]? Is it worth the retirement of Americans to subsidize Boeing, for instance? Are large corporate farmers worth more than America's poor elderly?

How Do We Assess Social Security's Record?

Social Security was long and widely hailed as the best and most successful government program. Now we know better. It is a program for its time, created when demographics camouflaged its inherent flaws. The program had the undoubted benefit of cutting rates of elder poverty, but at the cost of creating a fiscal time bomb that threatens to explode among generations in the coming years. Its adverse social consequences are many. Social Security—

- takes workers' money, making it harder for individuals to provide for themselves and their parents;

- weakens family and community ties;
- discourages work and saving;
- makes people more dependent on government;
- imposes enormous losses on workers in the name of security;
- threatens America's fiscal stability; and
- risks potential generational war as the system slides to ward insolvency.

Today we know the risks. But reform won't be easy. It is difficult enough to discuss Social Security. Toss in Medicare and, opines one political wit, "A good Medicare solution is more difficult than the war on terrorism, education, Social Security and homeland security combined." Toss in Medicaid, unemployment insurance, and some other programs and the task might seem hopeless.

Yet the third rail of politics failed in the 2006 election, despite the collapse of the presidential push for Social Security reform. Although Democrats were mostly against the reform, many recognized the problem even as they sought to score partisan points. Many Republicans were skittish of change, but it was Iraq, not Social Security, that cost the GOP Congress in November 2006.

In fact, from the late 1990s popular support for private accounts has held relatively steady. The strongest argument for many is not an arcane dispute over relative rates of return, but the very basic American value of self-reliance: Our retirement futures should be under our control, not that of self-interested politicians. The U.S. always has been notable as an ownership and opportunity society, and we need to rediscover those values. Reclaiming control of our retirement futures and putting the good of our families beyond that of irresponsible politicians in Washington is an important, and perhaps necessary, first step in doing so.

Until now neither party has been willing to confront the looming fiscal crisis resulting from the intersection of promised benefits for seniors and the growing population of seniors. To his credit, President George W. Bush raised the issue, but the possibility of reform was swept away in the crash of plans to democratize Mesopotamia. Now we seem to be back to dithering, and the longer we dither, the greater the budget problems and the harder the process of reform will become.

CHARLES MURRAY

Replacing the Welfare State with a Negative Income Tax on Steroids

Introduction

This essay is an abridgment of a short book titled *In Our Hands: A Plan to Replace the Welfare State* (Murray, 2006). Its argument can be reduced to a very short statement: America's population is wealthier than any in history. Every year, the American government redistributes more than a trillion dollars of that wealth to provide for retirement, health care, and the alleviation of poverty. We still have millions of people without comfortable retirements, without adequate health care, and living in poverty. Only a government can spend so much money so ineffectually. The solution is to give the money to the people.

The immediate reason for proposing a radical change in the welfare state is financial. No serious student of entitlements thinks that we can let the past trends in federal spending on health care continue. Social Security needs to be fixed with higher taxes or lower benefits. But the welfare state has a deeper fault line that ultimately will do more to bring about the welfare state's collapse than budgetary pressures.

The European and American welfare states evolved under the twin assumptions that resources were scarce and that government could allocate them effectively. The first assumption was true during the first half of the twentieth century, in this sense: No country had ever been so rich that its wealth, divided evenly among everyone, would provide everyone with a comfortable living. After World War II, in a few countries, wealth increased so much that, for the first time, there was enough money to go around. It was technically possible for no one to be poor. Much of the energy behind the social turmoil of the 1960s was fueled by this revolutionary change.

Enter the second assumption, that governments could allocate resources effectively. During the early decades of the welfare state, it seemed simple. The indigent elderly depend on charity, so let the government provide everyone with a guaranteed pension. The unemployed husband and father cannot find a job, so let the government give him some useful work to do and pay him for it. Some people who are sick cannot afford to go to a private physician, so let the government pay for health care.

It turned out not to be simple after all. The act of giving pensions increased the probability that people reached old age needing them. Governments had a hard time finding useful work for unemployed people and were ineffectual employers when they did. The demand for medical care outstripped the supply. But, despite the complications, these are the easy tasks. Scandinavia and the Netherlands—small, ethnically homogeneous societies, with traditions of work, thrift, neighborliness, and social consensus—do them best.

Traditions decay when the reality facing a new generation changes. The habit of thrift decays if there is no penalty for not saving. The work ethic decays if there is no penalty for not working. Neighborliness decays when neighbors are no longer needed. Social consensus decays with immigration. Even the easy tasks become hard as time goes on.

Then, during the second half of the twentieth century, the welfare state confronted accelerating increases in the number of people who were not just poor, but who behaved in destructive ways that ensured they would remain poor, sometimes living off their fellow citizens, sometimes preying on them. As their numbers grew, they acquired a new name: the underclass. The underclass grew first in the nation that was the largest and ethnically most heterogeneous: the United States. As the years passed, poor young men increasingly reached adulthood unprepared to work even when jobs were available. They were more disposed to commit crimes. Poor young women more often bore children without a husband. Poor children more often were born to parents who were incompetent to nurture them. When it came to solving these problems, it was obvious by the 1980s that government had failed. Then the evidence grew that government had exacerbated the problems it was trying to solve.

As Americans were making these discoveries, an underclass began to emerge in European welfare states also. That the easy tasks of the welfare state have become hard and underclasses are growing throughout the Western world are neither coincidences nor inevitable byproducts of modernity. The welfare state produces its own destruction. The process takes decades to play out, but it is inexorable. First, the welfare state degrades the traditions of work, thrift, and neighborliness that enabled a society to work at the outset; then it spawns social and economic problems that it is powerless to solve. The welfare state as we have come to know it is everywhere within decades of financial and social bankruptcy in Europe, and not far behind in America.

Radical change is ahead of us—not in the next election cycle, but eventually. What form should it take? Philosophically, I am a libertarian, and the libertarian solution is to prevent the government from redistributing money in the first place. But that is a solution that upward of 90 percent of the population will dismiss. Hence the proposal in *In Our Hands* is a sort of grand compromise between reality and my libertarian principles. The argument starts by accepting that the American government will continue to spend a huge amount of money on income transfers. It then contends that we should take all of that money and give it back to the American people in cash grants. Or to put it another way: I'll give you big government in terms of money if you'll give me small government in terms of the government's power to meddle in people's lives. The next steps are to explain how it might be done, why it is economically feasible, and the good that would follow.

The Plan

The provenance of the Plan—I have not been able to contrive a more memorable label for it—begins with the Negative Income Tax (NIT), an idea originated by Milton Friedman that attracted support among the Left in the 1960s.[1] To combat poverty, don't try to administer complicated welfare systems. Just give poor people the cash difference between what they make and the income necessary for a decent standard of living. During the 1970s, the federal government sponsored test versions of the NIT, most ambitiously in Denver and Seattle.

The NIT experiment produced disappointing results and convincingly demonstrated that a simple floor on income is a bad idea (Murray, 1984). But as the amounts of money that the United States spent on the poor continued to soar during the 1980s and 1990s, while poverty remained as high as it had been since the early 1970s, the underlying appeal of the NIT persisted: If we are spending that much money to eradicate poverty, why not just give poor people enough cash so that they won't be poor, and be done with it?

Friedman's concept was valid. The devil was in the details. A variant of the NIT puts it within our power to end poverty, provide for comfortable retirement and medical care for everyone, and, as a bonus that is probably more important than any of the immediate effects, to revitalize American civil society.

The Plan converts all transfer payments to a single cash payment for everyone age 21 and older. It would require a constitutional amendment that I am not competent to frame in legal language, but its sense is easy to express:

> Henceforth, federal, state, and local governments shall make no law nor establish any program that provides benefits to some citizens but not to others. All programs currently providing such benefits are to be terminated. The funds formerly allocated to them are to be used instead to provide every citizen with a cash grant beginning at age 21 and continuing until death. The annual value of the cash grant at the program's outset is to be $10,000.

Describing the Plan in the language of a constitutional amendment raises a host of practical political issues that I will ignore. All of these would be crucial if the nation started seriously considering the Plan, but we are stellar distances from that point. My limited proposition is that we are spending so much money on transfers that the Plan will surely be affordable by the time it could become a live political issue. Let's begin by thinking about whether that proposition is true.

The Plan does not require much in the way of bureaucratic apparatus. Its administration consists of computerized electronic deposits to bank accounts, plus resources to identify fraud. Here are the nuts and bolts:

Universal passport. At the Plan's adoption, each U.S. citizen receives a passport that has the same official status and uses as the current passport. Subsequently, a passport is issued to each U.S. citizen at birth. This passport also establishes eligibility for the grant.

A bank account. A condition of receiving the grant is that the citizen notify the government of an account at any U.S. financial institution with an American Bankers Association (ABA) routing number. The grant is electronically deposited into the account monthly. No bank account, no grant.

Reimbursement schedule. Earned income has no effect on the grant until that income reaches $25,000. From $25,000 to $50,000, a surtax is levied that reimburses the grant up to a maximum of $5,000. The surtax is 20 percent of incremental earned income (e.g., the tax at $30,000 is 20 percent of $30,000 minus $25,000, or $1,000).

Eligibility. The definition of earned income is based on individuals regardless of marital status or living arrangements. Thus, a wife who makes less than $25,000 will get the full $10,000, no matter how much her husband makes.

Changes in the size of the grant. As time goes on, even low inflation will erode the purchasing power of the grant. One option is to link its size to median personal earned income. Another is for Congress to make ad hoc adjustments to it, and a third is to link it to inflation. I leave the provision for adjusting the size of the grant open. The government's projections of the costs and benefits of maintaining the current system customarily assume zero inflation, and so will my projections of the costs and benefits of the Plan.

Tax revenues. The calculations assume that the tax system continues to generate revenue at the current rate, without specifying how the tax code might be changed. Whether current Social Security and Medicare taxes should remain as they are or whether the amounts of money they generate should be folded into individual or corporate taxes are separate issues that I do not try to address.

The programs to be eliminated. The Plan eliminates programs that are unambiguously transfers—Social Security, Medicare, Medicaid, welfare programs, social service programs, agricultural subsidies, and corporate welfare. It does not apply a strict libertarian definition of transfer, leaving activities such as state-funded education, funding for transportation infrastructure, and the post office in place. Services that are required for the operation of the courts and criminal justice system are also retained. For example, the enforcement of child-abuse laws sometimes means that children must be taken from their parents. Doing so requires that the government provide for the well-being of that child through facilities and services. A full list of the programs to be eliminated is given in Murray (2006: 130–39).

Basic Finances

A guaranteed minimum income of $10,000 a year for every adult American citizen is financially within our reach. By about 2011 it will be cheaper than maintaining the system now in place. I work through the numbers leading to that conclusion in the book (15–22, 140–47). Here, I will note briefly that in 2002, the year that will be the benchmark for all the financial calculations in this essay, the expenditures on the programs to be replaced by the Plan already amounted to the equivalent of about $6,900 for every man and woman in the United States age 21 or older. By now we are somewhere well over the $7,000 mark and rising fast.

As of 2002, the Plan could have been implemented with a $355 billion shortfall. I will not bother to consider ways of closing that gap through increased taxation or additional budget cuts because the gap will disappear on its own in a few years. Increases in the cost of the Plan will be much smaller than increases in the cost of the current system. The cost of the Plan will increase as the population increases and ages—about 1 percent per year in total spending (expressed as the compound average growth rate, CAGR, not the arithmetic average). But total government spending on the programs the Plan replaces will rise much faster. From 1980 to 2000, the annual real increase in the costs of the programs to be replaced averaged 2.9 percent, almost three times the rate of increase for the Plan.[2] Those increases are about to get larger, as the aging Baby Boomers generate increases in Social Security and Medicare far larger than those we saw in 1980 to 2000. Many analyses of this issue have been conducted. I have employed the budget projections prepared by the U.S. Congressional Budget Office (2003, 2004a, 2004b, 2005). The CBO projections for Social Security work out to an annual average increase of 3.6 percent, and the projections for Medicare work out to an annual average increase of 7.2 percent, compared to the annual 1 percent increase in the cost of the Plan.

A second reason for the disappearance of the gap is that the upper part of the income distribution keeps getting fatter, meaning that more and more people will pay back more and more of the grant as years go by, even if median income is stagnant, but I do not count on that in projecting costs of the Plan. The projection of costs for the current system uses a combination of budget forecasts by the Congressional Budget Office and extrapolations from past expenditures. The projection of the costs of the Plan, uses census projections for population by sex and age, applied to the income distribution by sex and age as of 2002. This projection assumes that the income distribution will remain unchanged—an upper bound for the cost of the Plan.

The projected costs of the current system and of the Plan cross in 2011. By 2020, the Plan would cost $549 billion less than a continuation of the current system. By 2028, the cost differential would be $1 trillion per year. This statement does not take transition costs into account. I discuss transition issues in the book (157–73). Here, I will simply note that a system that will cost a trillion dollars less than the current system per year by 2028 leaves a lot of wiggle room for dealing with transition costs.

Immediate Effects 1: Retirement

Most people are aware that Social Security is a bad deal as an investment for new entrants into this largest of Ponzi schemes, but a widespread impression persists that at least Social Security provides a floor for everyone that has nearly eliminated poverty among the elderly. Social Security does not accomplish even that much. As of 2002, 3.6 million elderly Americans were below the poverty line—more than one out of every ten people aged sixty-five and older, a rate only slightly lower than the poverty rate for the overall population (U.S. Bureau of the Census 2004a, table 2).

Social Security can leave so many people so poor because it is not universal and because the benefits for people who have worked only a portion of their adult lives are well below the poverty line. Thus the first advantage of the Plan over the current system: It is universal, and even in the worst case provides $10,000 a year for every elderly person in the country.

But the Plan does more than give everyone a guaranteed floor income. The Plan makes it possible for low-income people to have a comfortable retirement, not just get by. Summarizing the more detailed discussion in the text, consider someone who puts $2,000 a year in an index-based stock fund every year from age 21 until he retires at 66. What is the least he can expect to have when he retires? The Advisory Council to the Social Security Administration (SSA) in 1994–96 used an expected average real return of 6.5 percent in analyzing the three models for modifying Social Security that were presented to the President's Commission to Strengthen Social Security in 2001. The Congressional Budget Office (CBO) used 6.8 percent in analyzing the work of the commission. But let us be ridiculously conservative, first determining the worst compound average growth rate, using constant dollars, for any 45-year period in the history of the stock market: 4.3% from 1887 to 1932 (Siegel 1998). We then assume our 21-year-old will be the unluckiest investor in American history and get just a 4.0% average return. At the end of the 45-year period, he will have about $253,000, with which he could purchase an annuity worth about $20,500 a year.

This is with just a $2,000 annual contribution, equivalent to the Social Security taxes the government gets for a person making only $16,129 per year. The government extracts more than twice that amount from someone earning the median income, and more than five times that amount from the millions of people who pay the maximum FICA tax.

No matter how decisive the data on long-term returns from the stock market may be, many readers will not like the idea of letting people manage their own retirement plans without the backstop of Social Security. Here are my responses to the most common objections I have heard.

What about people who don't put anything away or invest their money unwisely? Everyone, including the improvident and incompetent who have squandered everything, still have $10,000 a year each, $20,000 per couple, no matter what. Six people who have completely squandered everything can pool their resources and have $60,000 per year, and so on. If a guaranteed floor is important, the Plan does a far better job than the current system.

What about shorter time periods? The 45-year time period is the correct one to use if the question is whether 21-year-olds should prefer the Plan or Social Security. But since many people defer their private saving for retirement until their 30s or later, it is important to note that the reliability of real returns remains high for shorter time periods. Consider, for example, the case of someone who waits until he is 36 to begin saving for retirement, giving him a 30-year investment period. There were 171 overlapping 30-year periods from 1802 to 2001. The worst of them still showed a profit, with a return of 2.7 percent (Siegel, 1998, for this and the following computations). In 163 of those 171 periods—95 percent of them—the average annual return was more than 4 percent. Even a person who has turned 51 and is looking at just a 15-year investment period should realize that out of the 186 such periods from 1802 to 2001, he would have lost money in only two of them (and then just barely), and would have averaged more than 4 percent in 148 of them (80 percent of the time).

What about the risks of trusting to the stock market versus the security of a government-backed guarantee? You have probably encountered an argument in the debate over proposals to privatize part of Social Security that goes something like this: "How can we rest the security of our elderly population on the vagaries of the stock market? No matter what the history of investments has been, we cannot be sure that the future will produce the same results. Better to maintain a system in which the government guarantees the result."

In the specific case of the Plan, a guarantee of $10,000 a year remains. But the larger fallacy in that argument needs to be more widely recognized. If stocks do not continue to appreciate in real value by an average of 4 percent over the next 45 years, the government will not be able to make good on its promises anyway. All of the government's promises depend on economic growth at least as robust as that implied by an anemic 4 percent average real return in the stock market. If we institute the Plan and the next generation happens upon a 45-year period so catastrophic that their retirement fund goes bust, the current system will have gone bust as well.

Immediate Effects 2: Health Care

Under the Plan, people will be responsible for their own health care, as they were from the founding of the republic until 1965, except that every adult, including all those who do not have health insurance under the current system, will now have $10,000 to tap for dealing with their health-care needs. Since health care is sui generis in a variety of ways, the discussion of this topic in *In Our Hands* is more extensive than for any other immediate outcome (37–51). But since the focus of this essay is the general proposition of a universal grant as a replacement for transfer payments, let me make the simplest of points about health care, and leave the complexities for discussion with those who wish to bring them up.

The Plan requires that every recipient of the grant, beginning at age 21, spends $3,000 of the $10,000 grant on a health-care insurance package that includes coverage for high-cost single events (e.g., an operation) and for catastrophic long-term illnesses or disability. The Plan also requires that insurance companies are required to treat the entire population as a single risk pool.[3] Given that situation, health insurance companies can offer a variety of plans with excellent coverage for somewhere around $3,000. They can be so inexpensive for the same reason that life insurance companies can sell generous life insurance cheaply if people buy it when they are young—the insurance company makes a lot of money from the annual payments before eventually having to write the big benefit checks. Providing access to basic medical care for everyone is easy for a country as rich as the United States—if we don't insist on doing it through the structure of the welfare state.

For the rest of the paper, I assume that $3,000 of the grant goes to health care from age 21 onward. I am not wedded to that precise number, however. The sense of the proposition is this: Figure out the cost of a no-frills, high-deductible insurance policy that would pay for extraordinary health care costs, including major surgery, all genetically based diseases, and illnesses involving long-term care or disability. That is the amount of money that I am willing for the government to provide. If it is discovered that the number is $3,800, then I will be happy to make the grant $10,800. The arguments in the rest of the essay assume $7,000 remains after health care is deducted. The main effect of tweaking the size of the grant would be to delay the crossover year when the Plan is no more costly than the current system.

Immediate Effects 3: Poverty

I conceive of poverty—meaning the lack of means to provide for basic material needs and comforts—along a dimension ranging from purely involuntary to purely voluntary. Involuntary poverty occurs when someone who plays by the rules is still poor. Poverty that I consider voluntary is the product of one's own idleness, fecklessness, or vice.

The immediate effect of the Plan is to end involuntary poverty. In a world where every adult starts with $10,000 a year, no one needs to go without decent food, shelter, or clothing. No one needs to do without most of the amenities of life, even when amenity is broadly defined. This statement holds even after taking the expenses of retirement and medical care into account. Abridging the more detailed calculations presented in the book (52–60), and assuming that $3,000 of the grant is devoted to health care (by requirement) and $2,000 is devoted to a retirement fund (voluntarily), leaving $5,000 per person per year, here is the story if we use the official poverty line as the definition for poverty.

A working-age individual living alone needs to work to escape poverty, but not very much, and not at a high-paying job. Someone could be out of work for more than six months and still reach the poverty threshold by working at a minimum-wage job. For a couple without children, one person could be completely unemployed, and the other work just 11 weeks in a course of a year, and the couple would still be over the poverty line. A couple with a child? If the father works at a minimum wage job, he can be unemployed for seven months out of the year and still reach the poverty line with a minimum-wage job, even though the mother doesn't work at all.

Surpassing the official poverty line under the Plan is easy for people in a wide range of circumstances, even in a bad economy, and even assuming jobs at the rock-bottom wage. To see how unrealistically stringent these conditions are, consider that the minimum wage I have been using is $5.15 an hour. The average janitor earned twice that—$10.28 an hour—in 2002 (U.S. Bureau of the Census, 2005b, table 620). Under the Plan, the average janitor working 40 hours a week for 48 weeks a year would have a total cash income of $24,738 plus health insurance and a retirement account. A janitor and a wife would have $29,738 plus health insurance and retirement accounts for both. The realistic effect of the Plan is not just to enable people to escape official poverty easily, but to escape poverty by even the most expansive definitions of the poverty line (e.g., half the median income).

Changes in benefits under the Plan versus the current system are not a one-way street. Many programs to help the poor would be gone: the earned income tax credit (EITC), temporary assistance for needy families (TANF, the cash payment that used to be called AFDC), food stamps, Medicaid, housing subsidies, and other programs. In net, which poor people would benefit under the Plan? Who would lose more than they gain?

The analysis in *In Our Hands* (56–57 and notes) demonstrates first that all low-income married or cohabiting couples in which at least one person works for a substantial portion of the year are better off under the Plan everywhere, children or no children. If neither the man nor the woman works at all—an extreme case indeed—the Plan is better for couples everywhere except the highest-benefit states, and even there it is a close call. Virtually all single, low-income males would benefit. The only exception is a single man with no income who has custody of children and who lives in a high-benefit state, a minuscule proportion of poor males.

The one major category of people who are better off financially under the current system is single mothers who have no earnings or low earnings, below or above age 21. Everywhere in the country, even in the low-benefit states, a case can be made that the total value of their benefits package is greater than $10,000. Theoretically, the Plan does not become clearly preferable for such women until earnings exceed $13,000 to $18,000, depending on the number of children and the state. I say "theoretically" because, under the current system, many women who qualify for benefits of this magnitude do not actually get them (many who legally qualify do not apply). In contrast, all single mothers will get the full $10,000 under the Plan.

I should also note that single mothers under the Plan do not need to live in poverty. First, they have the choice to work. If they work most of the year at a minimum-wage job, their earnings plus the grant get them out of poverty. In addition, a woman living under the Plan can get child support that is often unavailable under the current system—the father of her child has a monthly income arriving at a known bank account that can be tapped, and modern DNA analysis makes identification of the biological father easy (more on this presently).

But the greater availability of child support is only one of many new possibilities a single mother has for coping with her situation under the Plan. Even if a woman decides not to work but has $7,000 in cash to bring to the table, she can find some joint living arrangement with family or friends, or find some other group with whom to pool her resources. A single mother living in a world where she has the grant, and so do her family and friends, has a variety of ways to avoid poverty—by her own choices and actions, not by the dispensation of a bureaucracy.

Whether the paragraphs above are self-evidently true or unrealistically optimistic depends on one's premises about what human beings can be expected to do. Many observers on the Left argue that millions of people cannot be expected to go out and work at minimum-wage jobs or otherwise cope with daily life because of disadvantages they have suffered—racism, broken homes, poor education, poverty, and the like. I have just asserted that the number of people who cannot be expected to meet those standards is small.

I work from the premise that everyone not clinically retarded or mentally ill makes choices. Some people are able to make only the most basic choices, but one of those basic choices is whether to seek work and take it when offered. Another basic choice open to everyone is whether to behave cooperatively with family and neighbors. Conversely, failure to seek work or failure to behave cooperatively are choices. To deny that these are choices is to deny the humanity of the people we want to help. The fact that no able-bodied person needs to live in poverty doesn't mean that no one will live in poverty. Some people behave in ways that ensure they will live in squalor, will not have enough money to buy food, or will be evicted for not paying the rent. They may drink away their money or gamble it away. This kind of poor person we will indeed always have with us. The Plan ends involuntary poverty—the kind that exists when people have done the ordinary things right and are still poor. These are the people who most deserve help. Under the Plan, their poverty is ended.

Immediate Effects 4: The Underclass

The word underclass denotes a class of people who exist at the margins of American society. They are usually poor, but poverty is a less important indicator than personal behavior destructive to themselves and to their communities. Membership in the underclass is not a yes/no proposition, but for reasons I have discussed elsewhere (e.g., Murray, 1999), three categories of people constitute a large part of the problem: chronic criminals, never-married women with children, and able-bodied young men who are out of the labor force. How might the Plan affect them?

Criminality. According to sociological theory that sees crime as a response to economic deprivation, the Plan should reduce crime. The Plan will provide a nice test of such theories. But the twentieth century provided a nice test, too, and the theories flunked. Poverty fell; crime rose. The Plan may indirectly reduce crime through positive effects on family structure, but I will not forecast reduced crime as one of the Plan's positive effects. If it happens, it will be a bonus.

Births to Single Women. The Plan will plausibly produce a large reduction in births that occur to single women for the simplest of reasons: It introduces new penalties for nonmarital births for everyone involved.

The Plan obviously increases the economic penalty of having a baby for a single woman under 21, an age group that accounts for about one-third of all births to single women. The woman no longer gets any government assistance—no cash payment, no food stamps, no Medicaid, no housing subsidies, no subsidies for day care. The Plan also increases the economic penalty on the parents of a teenaged mother who is living at home. At present, the net financial effect on her parents is offset by the stream of benefits that accompanies the baby. Under the Plan, the costs of the new baby will fall on the girl's parents (in low-income neighborhoods, typically just her mother). The incentives to pressure the daughter to avoid pregnancy will increase.

The Plan increases the likelihood that the father of the child faces an economic penalty. Under the Plan, every man age 21 or older has a known income stream deposited to a known bank account every month. Police do not need to track him down or try to find him on a day when he has cash on hand. All they need is a court order to tap the bank account. Even teenaged fathers who are not yet getting the grant need not escape. Just write the child-support law so that their obligation accumulates until they turn 21, when he has to start paying it back.

For single women 21 and older, the major effect of the Plan is to create a cost of having a baby. Under the current system, the birth of a baby brings resources that would not be offered if the baby did not exist. Under the Plan, the baby will be a drain on resources. I frame the argument in the abstract, but it will not be abstract when the Plan goes into effect. Think in terms of a 20-year-old woman from a low-income neighborhood with a boyfriend. She knows she is about to start receiving a monthly check. She also knows women in her neighborhood who are already getting that check. The ones without babies are spending it on themselves. Her friends with babies are buying diapers and baby food, and probably living with their mothers because they cannot afford a place of their own. Under the Plan, the opportunity costs of having a baby will be obvious and alarming to low-income young women in the same way that they have always been obvious and alarming to middle-class and affluent young women.

Young Males Not in the Labor Market. The third category of people who embody the underclass is able-bodied young men in low-income neighborhoods who do not work or who do not even look for work. Through the middle of the twentieth century, such young males were rare. Since the middle of the 1960s, they have become common, especially among young black males. I will take 1999 as the example, at the height of the economic boom of the 1990s, when jobs were available everywhere in the country even for people with no job experience and no skills. Of males aged 16 to 24 who were not enrolled in school, 8 percent of whites and 22 percent of blacks were not working and not looking for work (unpublished tabulations from the Current Population Survey provided by the Bureau of Labor Statistics).

Some of these men live with parents. Some live with girlfriends. Many have income, but not from regular jobs. The money may come from crime, the gray market, or sporadic day-work. How will the Plan affect their behavior after they reach their 21st birthdays?

The Plan complicates their lives. It forces them to have an income, and one that other people know about. That fact produces a cascading set of consequences through what I call the Doolittle Effect, named after George Bernard Shaw's character in *Pygmalion* and, later, *My Fair Lady*, Alfred Doolittle—the one who, after being forced to have an income, discovers that he has to get to the church on time. The logic condensed comes down to this (see pages 66–70 in the book for the unabridged version).

Large numbers of young men who live with parents or girlfriends will find themselves under pressure to contribute for rent and food. Before the Plan, getting a low-paying job would merely bring those pressures upon them without providing enough money to move out and live on their own. Under the Plan, the pressures are unavoidable, but the combination of the grant plus the income from a low-paying job also makes it feasible to become independent. All those who, *ceteris paribus*, would prefer to be independent have gone from a situation in which they had little incentive to work to a situation in which they have substantial incentives to work.

It is hard to say whether the Doolittle Effect will include pressure on an unmarried father to marry the mother. In an age when cohabitation has become common, perhaps not, especially in states where child support can be enforced as easily against men who have never married the mother as against those who did. But pressures to act like a father will probably increase. A man with a steady income, as every man will have under the Plan, is treated differently from a man without a steady income. The fact of his income gives him a standing in others' calculations, including the assumption that a man can be pushed to shoulder responsibilities. I have no empirical basis for forecasting the proportions of idle young men who would fall in these various categories: Some will doubtlessly use the grant to continue being idle; for others the Doolittle Effect will be real. I cannot leave the discussion of effects on the underclass without alluding to a broader effect of the Plan that may be the most important of all. A persuasive critique of the current system is that the people who make up the underclass have no reason to think they can be anything else. They are poorly educated, without job skills, and living in neighborhoods where prospects are bleak. The quest for dignity and self-respect takes the form of trying to beat the system, whether the system means the criminal code or the rules that surround the distribution of welfare. The more fortunate members of society may see such people as obstinately refusing to take advantage of the opportunities that exist. Seen from the perspective of the man who has never held a job or the woman who wants to have an infant to love, those opportunities look fraudulent.

The Plan does not exhort the young man to go out and get a job. It does not urge the young woman to delay childbearing. It does not do anything that tries to stage-manage their lives. The Plan provides a stake—prospectively for those under 21, in actuality for those who have turned 21. The grant is not charity—everyone in the country turning 21 is getting the same thing. Seven thousand dollars of it consists of cash to be used as they wish, not little bundles of benefits to be allocated as the welfare bureaucracy sees fit. The grant is deposited monthly into that most middle-class of institutions, a bank account. The Plan says just one thing to people who have never had reason to believe it before: "Your future is in your hands." And it is the truth.

Immediate Effects 5: Work Disincentives

The most serious practical objection to the Plan is its potential effect on work. For years, economists have found through rigorous quantitative analysis what common sense predicts: Make it easier not to work and people work less. Unemployment insurance is the most obvious example, but almost any transfer payment linked to employment or wages has a work disincentive. To what extent will people stop working because of the cash grant, not to pursue some other equally productive life course, but to loaf?

The Plan does not even require such people to be sneaky. It says to 21-year-olds, "If half a dozen of you want to pool your grants, rent a cottage on an inexpensive beach, and surf for the rest of your lives, the American taxpayer will support you." The question is how many people are likely to respond to the grant in that way or, more broadly, how labor force participation and work effort might be expected to change. The discussion in *In Our Hands* works through a variety of scenarios (72–79). Here is where it comes out:

- Most of those who remain out of the labor force will be the same people who are out of the labor force under the current system.
- Most of the reductions in work effort will involve fewer hours worked, not fewer people working.
- Most of the people who leave the labor force will be college graduates who take time off between graduation and a permanent job or graduate school.
- The net decrease in work effort will be acceptable.

The key feature of the Plan that supports these conclusions is the high income level at which the grant begins to be paid back through the surtax ($25,000 of earned income). Past attempts to put a floor on income have foundered on very high marginal tax rates for low-income people getting the support who have the option of taking a job instead. Setting the start of the payback of the grant at $25,000 of earned income is an Alexandrian solution, cutting the knot rather than trying to untie it. It says, "Keep every cent you make until you reach $25,000, then we'll talk." By that time, it is too late to back out. If someone is earning $24,999 a year under the Plan, still getting the full grant, he is taking home a cash gross of $31,999. The surtax on the grant when he gets a raise to, say, $26,000 amounts to $200, leaving him with a cash gross of $32,800, compared to $7,000 if he stops working. The fact that someone starts paying a few hundred dollars in surtax when he first gets past $25,000 in earned income has no meaningful effect on his calculations about whether to continue working. A work disincentive may well be observed, but it will be concentrated in number of hours worked, not in the choice to work at all.

The Larger Purpose

I have set forth some ambitious claims for the immediate effects of the Plan. An end to involuntary poverty, universal health care, and universal access to comfortable retirements would not be trivial accomplishments. But, to my mind, they are secondary. Consider instead this completely different proposition: The real problem advanced societies face has nothing to do with poverty, retirement, health care, or the underclass. The real problem is how to live meaningful lives in an age of plenty and security.

Throughout history, much of the meaning of life was linked to the challenge of staying alive. Staying alive required being a contributing part of a community. Staying alive required forming a family and having children to care for you in your old age. The knowledge that sudden death could happen at any time required attention to spiritual issues.

Doing these things was a matter of necessity. But doing them also filled life with meaning in this most fundamental sense: People spent their lives doing important things with their time. The satisfactions associated with being a good spouse, good parent, good neighbor, and a productive member of the community were real, deep, and justified.

Life in an age of plenty and security requires none of the things that used to be part of staying alive. Being part of a community is not necessary. Marriage is not necessary. Children are not necessary. Attention to spiritual issues is not necessary. It is not only possible but easy to go through life with a few friends and serial sex partners, earning a good living, having a good time, and dying in old age with no reason to think that one has done anything more significant than while away the time.

Perhaps, as the song says, that's all there is. I disagree, and think that to live a human life means more than that. I have written an entire book on this (Murray, 1988), and *In Our Hands* spends several pages laying out the argument from that book (82–94). But for the purposes of this essay let me advance what is likely to be the most inflammatory proposition for this audience: Western Europe is the canary in the coal mine, warning us in America of what lies ahead if we emulate the European example. The phrase "an age of plenty and security" refers most accurately to Western Europe, which adopted the welfare state earlier than the United States and implemented it more completely. It was implemented earliest and most sweepingly in Germany, France, the Low Countries, and Scandinavia. Putting aside for a moment the budgetary crisis looming for these countries, they succeeded in their central goals. On almost any dimension of material well-being, those countries lead the world. Their indices of economic equality are the highest, and their indices of economic deprivation are the lowest. In the minds of many, the European welfare state represents the ideal America should emulate, a position recently expounded at length by Jeremy Rifkin (Rifkin, 2004).

In my view, the ideal represented by the European welfare state is suited only for a particular way of looking at human existence, one which holds that the purpose of life is to while away the time as pleasantly as possible, and the purpose of government to enable people to do so with as little effort as possible. It is reflected in what I will call the Europe Syndrome.

Europe's short work weeks and frequent vacations are one symptom of the Syndrome. The idea of work as a means to self-fulfillment has faded. The view of work as a necessary evil, interfering with the higher good of leisure, dominates. The Europe Syndrome also consists of ways in which vocation is impeded. Job security is high, but so is the danger that if you leave a job to seek a better one, you won't be able to find one. Starting a new business is agonizingly difficult. Elaborate restrictions impede employers from rewarding merit and firing the incompetent. The Europe Syndrome is dismissive of all the ways in which work can become vocation and vocation can become a central source of satisfaction in life.

The precipitous decline of marriage is another symptom. As fast as the marriage rate has dropped in the United States, by about a quarter since 1970, it is still 50 to 90 percent higher (depending on the country) than in the advanced welfare states of Western Europe (U.S. Bureau of the Census, 2005b, tables 70 and 1327). Part of the reason is direct: The advanced welfare state removes many of the traditional economic incentives to marry. But the larger reason involves the welfare state's effect on another reason for marriage: the desire to have children as a couple. The welfare state treats children as a burden to their parents that must be lightened through child allowances, subsidies, and services. The people of Europe have responded by agreeing. Children are no longer the central expression of a marriage and a life, but are objectified: Which to do—have a baby or buy a vacation home? Such is the calculus that young European adults routinely express when asked about their plans for children, and the value of the vacation home looms large. Why have a child when children are so expensive, so much trouble—and, after all, what good are they, really? Such are the attitudes that young European adults routinely express when asked why they have no children. And so, throughout Europe, fertility rates have fallen far below replacement level. This historically unprecedented phenomenon signifies more than a demographic trend. It reflects a culture of self-absorption—absorption not in some great ambition, but in the whiling away of life as pleasantly as possible.

The secularization of Europe is another symptom of the Europe Syndrome. Churches are empty. Europeans have broadly come to believe that humans are a collection of activated chemicals that, after a period of time, deactivate—nothing more. The causal arrow linking the welfare state and secularization could operate in either of two ways. If one believes there is no God and no transcendent meaning to life, then one might see the disappearance of religion in Europe as a valid consequence of the economic security that the welfare state has fostered. Human evolution led to religious beliefs as a psychological response for coping anxiety and misery. Take away the anxiety and misery, and religion falls away, too. Conversely, one may start by believing that God exists and life has transcendent meaning, but that the welfare state distracts humans from thinking about such things. Give people plenty and security, and they will fall into spiritual torpor. Whichever logic one employs, this unique secularization—no culture in recorded history has been nearly as secular as contemporary Europe's—cannot be blamed simply on modernity and economic wealth. Religion is alive and well in the United States. Secularization has occurred specifically in the advanced welfare states.

The same absorption in whiling away life as pleasantly as possible explains why Western Europe has become a continent with neither dreams of greatness nor the means to reacquire greatness. Europe's former scientific preeminence has vanished, as young scientists flock to American universities and corporations, even when they would prefer to live in their homelands, because they cannot hope for the professional freedom or financial support to pursue their work until they have crept up the bureaucratic chain. Even Europe's popular culture is largely borrowed from America, and its high culture can draw only on its glorious past—it has no contemporary high culture worthy of the name. All of Europe combined has neither the military force nor the political will to defend itself. The only thing Europe has left is economic size, and even that is growing at a slower pace than elsewhere. When life becomes an extended picnic, with nothing of importance to do, ideas of greatness become an irritant.

Such is the nature of the Europe Syndrome. The next issue is whether it is so awful. What is wrong with a society in which everyone one can while away life as pleasantly as possible? In its barest form, my position is that the number of institutions through which a satisfying life can be constructed are quite limited. Confining ourselves to the secular, there are really just three: vocation, family, and community. Seen in that light, one of the chief functions of government in enabling its citizens to construct satisfying lives for themselves is to ensure the vitality of those three institutions. How would the Plan interact with this core function of government?

The Plan and Vocation

I use vocation to label what others might call self-fulfillment. A central satisfaction of life comes from the sense of doing something one values, and doing it well. A few people know early in their lives that they are called to a vocation, whether to be priests or cellists or farmers or mothers. More commonly, people come to a vocation by trial and error. The role the Plan plays is twofold. The Plan makes it easier to find a vocation by changing jobs, and easier for a person to accumulate the capital to pursue a dream.

Few teenagers finish high school already knowing what job will make them happy. The process of finding a job that makes one happy often continues well into a person's 20s and often beyond. Only for a lucky few does it mean finding the perfect job. Jobs vary along many dimensions, and the history of most people who find satisfaction in a job is one of incrementally improving their situation over a period of years. This typically has meant changing employers and moving geographically.

Europe is especially useful as the canary in this part of the coal mine. Government regulation has made the costs of hiring an employee so high, and made it so hard to dismiss an employee, that the European labor market has become rigid. New jobs are scarce, and long-term unemployment is high. So an employee who has a job he hates nonetheless will tend to keep it. European peasants used to be tied to the land. In this new version of serfdom, European workers are tied to their jobs.

A major strength of the American economy is its history of high labor mobility. As in other aspects of the welfare state, however, the United States is on the European track. The Plan does nothing about one of the main sources of increasing immobility—the regulatory mandates that increasingly constrain the hiring and firing process—but it does promote freedom to move from job to job. The main effect follows from the widespread reductions the Plan will produce in job-related medical coverage and retirement plans. Under the Plan, millions more people will have portable retirement accounts and medical insurance. By the same token, the freedom of millions more people to look for a better job will be increased, and this is an essential part of incrementally finding a vocation.

The same effect will be felt by people who are out of the labor market altogether. Consider a single mother who has successfully gotten TANF, housing assistance, Medicaid, and food stamps in a city where the job market is bad. For her to pull up stakes and move to a city where the job market is better is foolish. If she doesn't find a job, she will have to go through the whole uncertain and stressful application process again and survive all its delays before she begins to get renewed support. Under the Plan, she faces none of those costs. Government no longer ties her to a place. The Plan also gives people a way to accumulate enough money to try to realize their ambitions—to go to college after all, even though they have a family to support; to start their own business; to pull up stakes and move to Alaska. The dreams can take numberless variations, but people working in low-income jobs and responsible for families usually have to abandon them. The Plan does not make such dreams easy to realize, but it does bring them into the realm of the possible, given discipline and hard work.

That last proviso—"given discipline and hard work"—points to one of the ways in which the Plan is likely to have positive side effects. The Plan does not provide enough money in any one year to finance much of anything. It does provide enough money so that someone can save over the course of three or four years, then go to the bank and say, "Here is what I have done, planning for this day, and how much I have accumulated," and thereby have a chance of getting a loan. That prospect and the experience of saving over those years are themselves valuable outcomes. The Plan will expand that prospect to millions of people who have never considered it before. Within those millions, some subset will acquire habits of self-discipline and long-term planning that will positively affect their lives on many dimensions. And, not incidentally, many within that subset will succeed in achieving their original dream.

The Plan and Family

The effects of the Plan on the decision to marry could be large or small, depending on the legal importance of marriage in determining rights and obligations regarding children. The trend for many years has been to blur the legal distinction between marriage and cohabitation. Given that trend, I expect the effects on the decision to marry to be small, for reasons discussed in the book (101–3).

Whatever happens to the laws surrounding marriage, large numbers of people will continue to get married. The effects of the Plan on the married are of four kinds: effects on divorce; effects that make it easier for mothers to have both children and a career; effects that make it easier for mothers to stay at home; and effects that increase the autonomy and responsibility of the family as a unit.

Effects on divorce. Under the current system, women who forgo careers to be full-time housewives and mothers are vulnerable to being forced into the labor market in mid-life without job skills or experience. For affluent couples, this vulnerability is counterbalanced by adequate alimony and child support. The Plan provides a similar counterbalance for women in low-income and middle-income households. One may be opposed to divorce and yet in favor of measures that free women from the economic compulsion to remain in a bad marriage. On the other side of the ledger, the Plan's financial guarantee will make it easier for salvageable marriages to break up. I know of no way to forecast what the mix will be.

Effects that make it easier for mothers to have both children and a career. As I tackle the delicate topic of whether mothers stay at home or have a job outside the home, the crucial distinction is between mothers who work because they like their jobs and those who work out of economic necessity. For now, I am referring exclusively to mothers who prefer to work outside the home.

Mothers in affluent households who want to work outside the home hire nannies or send their children to good day-care centers. The Plan makes it easier for mothers in low-income and middle-income households to do the same thing. For families in which the woman is already working, the Plan will ease the financial strain of paying for child care. For families in which the woman is not working but wants to, the Plan will enable her to do so by providing resources for buying child care. I interpret both effects as being good for the marriages in question. The Plan does nothing to persuade mothers with children to work outside the home. It makes it easier for them to do so if they want to.

Effects that make it easier for mothers to stay home. Now the issue is the mother who is working out of economic necessity, but, given the option, would rather work part-time or be a full-time housewife and mother. Once again, the Plan is not going to affect the decisions of women in affluent households for whom the grant is a negligible percentage of the family's income. But the Plan is likely to have large effects on households with incomes well into the middle class. For many women with young children who work only because they have to help make ends meet, the grant can easily represent the difference between financial hardship and being able to get along on the husband's income alone. Insofar as the Plan permits more women to do what they prefer to do regarding a central life role—mother—it is unambiguously positive for those women and positive for the children as well. More mothers staying at home because they choose to do so will also be good for marriage. A marriage can be filled with family activities, or it can be stripped down. The more time that is filled by careers, the more stripping-down of family life has to occur. It is not a matter of choice. Weekends are a different kind of experience in a family where all the domestic chores of the week must be crowded into Saturday and Sunday versus one where they are not. The availability for volunteer work at the local school differs between those two households. The availability to be a neighbor in times of need differs. The availability to care for aging parents differs. The availability to be a deacon in one's church differs. All of these activities on the part of either parent are in addition to the childrearing activities that can fill a marriage or be stripped down. It is a simple relationship: The more resources that are devoted to a marriage, the richer that marriage is likely to be. The richer the marriages in a community, the more the community thrives. The Plan's effect on enabling wives to stay home if they wish could be one of its most important ones.

Effects that make the family more autonomous and responsible. The Plan returns core functions and responsibilities to the family, and doing so is likely to have a revitalizing effect on the institution as a whole.

Consider this paradox: Taking on a wife and then becoming a father is what a young man, full of wild oats, should least like to do. And yet throughout history and across cultures, young men have yearned to marry. Why have young men so consistently acted against what their hormones would lead them to do in a state of nature? The direct answer is that marriage used to be the only way that most men could get regular sexual access to a woman—a powerful incentive. But that is only part of the explanation. Over the eons required for us to become Homo sapiens, humans living in demanding environments had a survival advantage if the man stuck around after he impregnated a woman, suggesting that by this time, a male's genetic makeup contains predispositions not only to sow wild oats, but also to be a family man. Whether he ever becomes a family man depends on how culture mediates these competing impulses.

Historically, culture has taken the incentives I just described and pieced together a narrative around them consisting of norms, rewards, and punishments. In the case of young males, most cultures provided for a period of sowing wild oats but also said to them that the way to enter the fraternity of men was by becoming a husband and father. That message was based on a truth: The welfare of the community depended upon the formation of stable families. Being a husband and father became the badge of being an adult male because those roles were laden with responsibilities and obligations.

Now consider the phrase that is so often applied to social welfare systems: the safety net. It is wonderfully apt. People who know that a net is below them do reckless things that they wouldn't do otherwise. Under the current system, the net is there regardless of how people behave. Under the Plan, people have ample raw materials for a net, but they must weave it for themselves. People have to make choices, and it is possible to make the wrong choices. The potential rewards from marriage increase for low-income men and women, because the economic assets they bring to the marriage increase. Each partner brings resources that, combined and used prudently, give them the prospect of a bright and secure future. Similarly, the potential risks increase: Men and women alike have more to lose economically if their prospective spouses are irresponsible. I do not mean to sound naive. People have made bad marriage choices throughout history and will continue to do so under any regime. But the Plan restores some of the traditional narrative that in the past led people to look beyond short-term sexual attraction and think about long-term effects.

Under the Plan, everyone still has the option to remain single, moving in and out of relationships. But most people want something deeper and more lasting than that, something that looks like marriage traditionally defined. Under the Plan, marriage once again becomes the locus within which a man and woman can make a future together, laden with responsibilities and obligations that cannot be put aside.

The Plan and Community

The effects of the Plan on vocation and family will be substantial, but the effects on civil life will be transforming. As the government's role in American life spread during the last 70 years, it crowded out America's most effective resource for dealing with human needs. The Plan returns the stuff of life to the hands of civil society.

Here is Alexis de Tocqueville on the American genius for voluntary association:

> Americans of all ages, all stations in life, and all types of dispositions are forever forming associations. There are not only commercial and industrial associations in which all take part, but others of a thousand different types—religious, moral, serious, futile, very general and very limited, immensely large and very minute. Americans combine to give f'tes, found seminaries, build churches, distribute books, and send missionaries to the antipodes. Hospitals, prisons, and schools take place in that way. Finally, if they want to proclaim a truth or propagate some feeling by the encouragement of a great example, they form an association. In every case, at the head of any new undertaking, where in France you would find the government or in England some territorial magnate, in the United States you are sure to find an association. (Tocqueville ([1835] 1969: 513)

The tradition continues today, evident in private philanthropic endeavors that are much rarer in Europe, and in the continuing social and religious organizations that are still an important part of life in working-class and middle-class America. But much has changed as well, for reasons that Tocqueville anticipated:

> A government could take the place of some of the largest associations in America, and some particular states of the Union have already attempted that. But what political power could ever carry on the vast multitude of lesser undertakings which associations daily enable American

citizens to control? . . . The more government takes the place of associations, the more will individuals lose the idea of forming associations and need the government to come to their help. That is a vicious circle of cause and effect. (Tocqueville ([1835] 1969: 515, 517)

The simple number of associations continues to increase to this day. But the newcomers are no longer associations that take on social tasks for themselves. Rather, they are advocacy groups that seek to influence how the government will do those tasks (Skocpol, 2003: 127–74). The experience of voluntary associations based on broad memberships that actually performed the social tasks vindicated Tocqueville's prediction. They were still growing into the 1920s. Then their membership declined precipitously (Skocpol, 2003: 55).

This is not the place to untangle all the ways in which changes in American society affected voluntary associations, but two large events are among them. First came the 1935 Social Security Act, which created both Social Security and Aid to Families with Dependent Children. Each program took what had been a major arena of private activity unto the federal government. Thirty years later came Lyndon Johnson's Great Society and the proliferation of social programs that accompanied it, proclaiming in effect that there was no longer any aspect of poverty and deprivation that the federal government would not take the lead in solving.

To convey what has been lost, it is necessary to tell the story of how extensive civic participation used to be. It begins with the network of fraternal associations for dealing with misfortune or old age through mutual insurance, such as the Odd Fellows, Elks, Masons, Moose, Redmen, and Knights of Pythias. Some were organized around specific occupations. Some were linked to membership in an ethnic group—Hebrew, Irish, Italian. Most of the associations run by whites excluded blacks in those years, but that did not keep blacks from just as energetically developing their own fraternal associations. In the latter part of the nineteenth century, for example, the highest ratio of Odd Fellows lodges per 100,000 population was found among northern blacks (Skocpol, 2003: 55). In combination with black churches, the fraternal organizations constituted the social backbone of black communities that were far healthier in their family structure and social norms than black communities in today's inner cities.[4]

Few people today realize the size and reach of these networks. In the mid-1920s, the National Fraternal Congress had 120,000 lodges (Beito, 2002: 197). The Odd Fellows had about 16 million members and the Knights of Pythias about 6 million (Skocpol, 2003: 90). Today, the remnants of these fraternal organizations perform shadows of their former functions. Besides their mutual insurance functions, the fraternal organizations supported extensive social service activities. In that task they were supplemented by a long list of other charities exclusively focused on assistance to nonmembers. It is difficult to convey the magnitude of the effort to help the poor prior to the advent of the welfare state because that effort was so decentralized, but consider just a few statistics from New York City at the turn of the twentieth century. Here is the roster of activities discovered in a survey of 112 Protestant churches in Manhattan and the Bronx: 48 industrial schools, 45 libraries or reading rooms, 44 sewing schools, 40 kindergartens, 29 small-sum savings banks and loan associations, 21 employment offices, 20 gymnasia and swimming pools, 8 medical dispensaries, 7 full-day nurseries, and 4 lodging houses (Olasky, 1992: 86).

Those are just some of the Protestant churches in two boroughs of New York City, and it is not a complete list of the activities shown in the report. Now suppose I could add (I do not have the data) the activities in the other boroughs. Then add the activities of the rest of the Protestant churches. Then add the activities of the New York Catholic diocese. Then add those of the Jewish charities. And, after all that, suppose I could tally the activities of a completely separate and extensive web of secular voluntary associations. The scale of voluntary activity in coping with human needs was huge.

If the question is whether such philanthropic networks successfully dealt with all the human needs that existed, the answer is obviously no. Dire poverty existed in the presence of all this activity. But that is not the right question. The assistance was being given in the context of national wealth that in 1900 amounted to per capita gross domestic product (GDP) of about $5,400 in today's dollars, and about two-thirds of the nation's nonfarm families were below the poverty line as presently defined.[5] I must put it as an assertion because the aggregate numbers for philanthropy in New York City cannot be accurately estimated, but I think it is a safe assertion: New York City's tax base in 1900 could not have funded anything approaching the level of philanthropic activities—cash and services combined—that were provided voluntarily. The correct question to ask about dealing with human needs in the twenty-first century is: What if the same proportional level of effort went into civil society's efforts to deal with human needs at today's level of national wealth?

I urge interested readers to pursue the story of the voluntary associations—they represent an extraordinary, largely forgotten accomplishment. At the time the New Deal began, mutual assistance for insurance did not consist of a few isolated workingmen's groups. Philanthropy to the poor did not consist of a few Lady Bountifuls distributing food baskets. Broad networks, engaging people from the top to bottom of society, spontaneously formed by ordinary citizens, provided sophisticated and effective social insurance and social services of every sort. They did so not just in rural towns or small cities, but in the largest and most impersonal of megalopolises. When I express confidence that under the Plan such networks will regenerate, it is based on historical precedent about how Americans left to themselves tackle social needs, not on wishful thinking.

This leaves open the question of whether it is better to let civil society handle these efforts. It may be argued that it is better to have paid bureaucracies deal with social problems. That way, the burden is not left to people who choose to help, but shared among all the taxpayers. Furthermore, it is more convenient to have bureaucracies do it. Being a part-time social worker appeals to some people, but most of us would rather pay our taxes and be done with it. Perhaps we should concentrate on improving the government bureaucracies that deal with these problems, not dismantling them.

The benefits of returning these functions to civil society are of two kinds: Benefits for the recipients of assistance and benefits for the rest of us.

The Benefits for Recipients. People trying to help those in need must struggle with the dilemma of moral hazard. People who are in need through no fault of their own can be given generous assistance with no downside risk. But people who are in need at least partly because of their own behavior pose a problem: How to relieve their distress without making it more likely that they will continue to behave in the ways that brought on their difficulties, and without sending the wrong signal to other people who might be tempted?

Bureaucracies have no answer to this dilemma. They cannot distinguish between people who need a pat on the back and those who need a stern warning. They cannot provide help to people who have behaved irresponsibly in a way that does not make it easier for others to behave irresponsibly. Bureaucracies, by their nature, must be morally indifferent. Indeed, the advocates of the welfare state hold up the moral neutrality of the bureaucracy as one of its advantages because aid is provided without stigma. In contrast, not only are private organizations free to combine moral instruction with the help they give, but such moral instruction is often a primary motivation for the people who are doing the work. Religious belief is sometimes its basis, but the point of view emerges in secular organizations as well. If the recipients of the help are approached as independent moral agents, and if their behavior has contributed to their problems, then the provision of assistance must be linked with attempts to get them to change their ways, subtle or overt. The result is that private philanthropies tend to provide help in ways that minimize moral hazard. Sometimes moral hazard is reduced because a social penalty accompanies the help. Sometimes moral hazard is reduced because the outlook and behavior of the person receiving the assistance is changed for the better. In either case, private charities have the advantage over bureaucracies if the objective is not just to minister to needs, but to discourage the need from arising.

Bureaucracies are also inferior to private philanthropy because a bureaucracy's highest interest cannot help being its own welfare. A new employee may enter a bureaucracy as idealistic as any volunteer, but those who thrive and advance will be those who advance the bureaucracy's interests most effectively. In the business sector, that means growing by gaining new customers and being profitable. For a government bureaucracy, it means growing by increasing its budget and staff. The institutional interests that drove private philanthropy before the government took a role were the opposite. Charitable organizations had to attract volunteers and donors. Private charitable organizations had no choice but to keep the effectiveness of their work at the forefront of their attention, else they would go out of business.

It is possible to destroy these advantages of private organizations. The United Way seems designed to make supporting charitable services as much like paying taxes as possible. Go to the Ford Foundation, Red Cross, or other philanthropies with large guaranteed incomes, and you will usually find splendid executive offices, bloated administrative staffs, and layers of paperwork. Go instead to the Salvation Army or any philanthropy that relies on volunteers and a steady stream of small incoming donations, and you will tend to find lean administrative staffs and a continuing focus on the recipients of the assistance.

The Benefits for the Rest of Us. The second large benefit of taking these functions back into our own hands is that turning them over to a bureaucracy means turning over too much of the stuff of life to them. By "stuff of life" I mean the elemental events of birth, death, growing up, raising children, comforting the bereaved, celebrating success, dealing with adversity, applauding the good, and scorning the bad—coping with life as it exists around us in all its richness. The chief defect of the welfare state from this perspective is not that it is inefficient in dealing with social needs (though it often is), nor that it is ineffectual in dealing with them (though it often is), nor even that it often exacerbates the very problems it is supposed to solve (as it often does). The welfare state drains too much of the life from life.

This argument is not an exhortation for us all to become social workers in our spare time. Give the functions back to the community, and enough people will respond. Free riders can be tolerated. Rather, the existence of vital, extensive networks of voluntary associations engaged in dealing with basic social needs benefits all of us for two other reasons.

The first reason is that such networks are an indispensable way for virtue to be inculcated and practiced in the next generation, and the transmission of virtue is the indispensable task of a free society that lasts.

The link between virtue and the success of a free society is not theoretical, but tangible and immediate. A free market cannot work unless the overwhelming majority of the population practices good faith in business transactions. Allowing people to adopt any lifestyle they prefer will not work if a culture does not socialize an overwhelming majority of its children to take responsibility for their actions, to understand long-term consequences, and to exercise self-restraint. Ultimately, a free society does not work unless the population shares a basic sense of right and wrong based on virtue classically understood, propounded in similar terms by thinkers as culturally dissimilar as Aristotle and Confucius. As Edmund Burke put it, "Men are qualified for civil liberty in exact proportion to their disposition to put moral chains upon their own appetites. . . . It is ordained in the eternal constitution of things that men of intemperate minds cannot be free. Their passions forge their fetters" (Burke, 1791).

The question then becomes how virtue is acquired. Aristotle's answer is still the right one: Virtue has the characteristics of a habit and of an acquired skill. It is not enough to tell children that they should be honest, compassionate, and generous. They must practice honesty, compassion, and generosity in the same way that they practice a musical instrument or a sport. Nor does the need for practice stop with childhood. People who behave honestly, compassionately, and generously do not think about each individual choice and decide whether in this particular instance to be honest, compassionate, or generous. They do it as a habit.

If this is an accurate description of how virtue is acquired, then transferring human problems to bureaucracies has an indirect consequence that ultimately degrades the society as a whole: Doing so removes the arena in which virtues such as generosity and compassion are practiced. It may not be necessary for everyone to become a volunteer social worker to find satisfaction in life, but it is important that people deal with the human needs of others in a way that is an integral part of everyone's life. In a society where the responsibility for coping with human needs is consigned to bureaucracies, the development of virtue in the next generation is impeded. In a society where that responsibility remains with ordinary citizens, the development of virtue in the next generation is invigorated.

The other reason that the stuff of life should not be handed over to bureaucracies involves the dynamics through which communities remain vital or become moribund. Broken down into constituent parts, vital communities consist of a multitude of affiliations—people who are drawn to engage with one another. Some of these affiliations are as simple as shopping at a local store, some are intended for nothing more than a good time—the backyard barbecue. Some are organizational—being part of the PTA. The kinds of affiliations that draw communities together and give them vitality are tendrils that require something to attach themselves to, some core of functions around which the affiliations that constitute a vital community can form and grow. When the government takes away a core function, it takes away one of the poles for those tendrils. By hiring professional social workers to care for those most in need, it cuts off nourishment to secondary and tertiary behaviors that have nothing to do with social work. According to the logic of the social engineer, there is no causal connection between such apparently disparate events as the establishment of a welfare bureaucracy and the reduced likelihood (after the passage of some years) that, when someone dies, a neighbor will prepare a casserole for the bereaved family's dinner. According to the logic I am using, there is a causal connection of great importance. These are my reasons for thinking that the effects of the Plan on civic life will be transforming. The grant will put in each individual's hands the means to take care of himself under ordinary circumstances. But some will not take care of themselves. Sometimes the reasons will be beyond their control. Sometimes their misfortunes will be their own fault. Most reasons will be somewhere in between. The responses to the needs posed by these cases will be as flexible as their causes. The level of wealth available to address these needs will dwarf the resources that were available to the fraternal and philanthropic networks of a century ago. Nothing stands in the way of the restoration of networks that are appropriate and generous, and that actually solve problems, except the will to put the responsibility for those problems back in our hands.

Conclusion

I began this thought experiment by asking you to ignore that the Plan was politically impossible. I end it by proposing that something very like the Plan is politically inevitable—not next year, but sometime. Two historical forces lead me to this conclusion.

The first is the secular increase in wealth as the American economy keeps on growing. Here is the history of American GDP since 1900.

Real per-capita GDP has grown with remarkable fidelity to an exponential growth equation for more than a century. It is, of course, possible to elect leaders so incompetent that they will do to the American economy what the Soviet leaders did to theirs, but, short of that, we are probably going to watch wealth increase in the decades to come. That curve cannot keep going up for much longer without it becoming obvious to a consensus of the American electorate that lack of money cannot be the reason we have poverty, lack of medical coverage, or an underclass. The problem is that we are spending the money badly. The second great historical force is the limited competence of government—not our government in particular, or the welfare state in particular, but any government. The limits do not arise because bureaucrats are lazy or the laws improperly written, but from truths about what human beings do when they are not forced to behave in ways that elicit the voluntary cooperation of other people. If constructed with great care, it is possible to have a government that administers a competent army, competent police, and competent courts. Even accomplishing this much is not easy. Comparatively few governments in the world's history have succeeded. Every step beyond these simplest, most basic tasks is fraught with increasing difficulty. By the time the government begins trying to administer to complex human needs, it is far out of its depth. Individuals and groups acting privately, forced to behave in ways that elicit the voluntary cooperation of other people and groups, do these jobs better. The limited competence of government is inherent. At some point in this century, that, too, will become a consensus understanding.

Once enough people recognize these realities, the way will be open for reform. What was clear to the Founders will once again become clear to a future generation: The greatness of the American project was that it set out to let everyone live life as each person saw fit, as long as each accorded the same freedom to everyone else.

America could not reach that goal as long as the fatal flaw of slavery persisted. When the goal came into sight in the 1960s, we lost our focus and then lost ground. Sometime in the twenty-first century it will become possible to take up the task again, more expansively than the Founders could have dreamed but seeking the same end: taking our lives into our own hands—ours as individuals, ours as families, and ours as communities.

Notes

1. The idea was first broached in Stigler (1946). Stigler revealed that the idea came from Milton Friedman in later correspondence (Burkhauser and Finegan, 1993: 128). Friedman's best-known discussion of the NIT is Friedman (1962): 191–94. An early example of the Left's interest in the NIT is Lampman (1965).
2. Murray (2006: 140–47) describes the data sources and methods. If the time period chosen were 1990–2000, the corresponding CAGR would be 3.1 percent. If the time period were 1970–2000, it would be 4.5 percent. My use of the 2.9 percent CAGR from 1980–2000 is a conservative basis for stating the historical cost increases of the programs to be replaced. The same statement applies if per capita increases in real costs are used instead of total increases in real costs.
3. This represents a revision of the Plan as presented in *In Our Hands*, where I propose the single risk pool as one of three optional reforms. I now consider it to be an essential part of the scheme.
4. Along with a greater appreciation of the size and effectiveness of voluntary associations, we badly need wider appreciation of the health and resilience of black institutions and the black family prior to the New Deal, in the face of socio-economic oppression and legal discrimination unimaginable today. For a classic account of the role of these institutions, see DuBois ([1899] 1967). For an account of the black family before the welfare state, see Gutman (1976).

5. In 2002 dollars, the average annual earnings in 1900 for all occupations was about $9,500; in nonfarm occupations, about $10,600 (U.S. Bureau of the Census [1975]: D779–D793), which typically had to support a family with at least two children, usually more. The poverty threshold for a family of four in 2002 was $18,244.

References

Beito, D. T. 2000. *From Mutual Aid to the Welfare State: Fraternal Societies and Social Services, 1890–1967*. Chapel Hill, NC: University of North Carolina Press.

Burke, E. 1791. *Letter to a Member of the National Assembly. In The Maxims and Reflections of Burke*, ed. F. W. Rafferty, http://www.ourcivilisation.com/smartboard/shop/burkee/maxims/chap18.htm (accessed October 4, 2005).

Burkhauser, R. V., and T. A. Finegan. 1993. "The Economics of Minimum Wage Legislation Revisited." *Cato Journal* 13 (1): 123–29.

DuBois, W. E. B. [1899] 1967. *The Philadelphia Negro: A Social Study*. New York: Benjamin Blom.

Friedman, M. 1962. *Capitalism and Freedom*. Chicago: University of Chicago Press.

Gutman, H. G. 1976. *The Black Family in Slavery and Freedom 1750–1925*. New York: Vintage Books.

Lampman, R. 1965. "Approaches to the Reduction of Poverty." *American Economic Review* 55:521–29.

Murray, C. 1984. *Losing Ground: American Social Policy 1950–1980*. New York: Basic Books.

_____. 1988. *In Pursuit: Of Happiness and Good Government*. New York: Simon and Schuster.

_____. 1999. *The Underclass Revisited*. Washington, DC: AEI Press.

_____. 2006. *In Our Hands: A Plan to Replace the Welfare State*. Washington, DC: AEI Press.

Olasky, M. 1992. *The Tragedy of American Compassion*. Washington, DC: Regnery Gateway.

Rifkin, J. 2004. *The European Dream: How Europe's Vision of the Future is Quietly Eclipsing the American Dream*. New York: Penguin.

Siegel, J. 1998. *Stocks for the Long Run: The Definitive Guide to Financial Market Returns and Long-Term Investment Strategies*, 2nd ed. New York: McGraw-Hill, Updated through 2001 at http://www.jeremysiegel.com (accessed October 4, 2005).

Skocpol, T. 2003. *Diminished Democracy: From Membership to Management in American Life*. Norman, OK: University of Oklahoma Press.

Stigler, G. 1946. "The Economics of Minimum Wage Legislation." *American Economic Review* 36 (June): 358–65.

Tocqueville, A. [1835] 1969. *Democracy in America*. Trans. G. Lawrence. Garden City, NY: Anchor Books.

U.S. Bureau of the Census. 1975. *Historical Statistics of the United States, Colonial Times to 1970*, vol. 1. Washington, DC: U.S. Bureau of the Census.

_____. 2005a. "Historical Income Tables." In *Current Population Survey*. Annual social and economic supplement, http://www.census.gov/hhes/income/histinc/p54.html (accessed October 4, 2005).

_____. 2005b. *Statistical Abstract of the United States 2004–2005*, http://www.census.gov/prod/www/statistical-abstract-04.html (accessed October 4, 2005).

U.S. Congressional Budget Office. 2003. *Evaluating and Accounting for Federal Investment in Corporate Stocks and Other Private Securities*. Washington, DC: Congress of the United States.

_____. 2004a. *The Budget and Economic Outlook: An Update*. Washington, DC: Congress of the United States.

_____. 2004b. *The Outlook for Social Security*. Washington, DC: Congress of the United States.

_____. 2005. *Budget Options*. Washington, DC: Congress of the United States.

STEPHEN MOORE

Disaster Relief as
an Entitlement

The question we need to ask is, "What happened?" What happened to the Republican Revolution?

Didn't the Republican Party learn from the Democrats? The Democrats had been thrown out of Washington for being big spenders, for running up the budget every year, for losing control of the purse strings. So we put Republicans in charge, confident they would get control of our federal fiscal resources. Ten years later it appears that the Republicans have become just like the Democrats. What happened?

The results of the 2006 election had been in process for five or six years. That was because the Republicans had lost their brand, the brand being that they were the party of limited government, fiscal responsibility, and lower taxes. This brand had been pay dirt for the Republican Party for the past 25 years, ever since Ronald Reagan came into office. Republicans won virtually every presidential election in the past 25 years, except for Bill Clinton's two terms. This image had been the Republican magic—being the party of less government and lower taxes. That has been squandered over the past six years.

Look at overall government spending during the last five years. George W. Bush has been in office since 2001. He has enacted six budgets. Over that time, the federal budget has grown 49.6%. True, a lot of that growth is a result of the war on terror. More money has had to be spent on homeland security and national defense.

To argue that this happened because of the events of September 11, 2001, is simply false. It turns out that national defense spending hasn't grown any faster than domestic social welfare spending over the last six years. The fastest growing agencies of the federal government during that time have not been the Department of Defense or even Homeland Security.

When President Reagan came into office he said he was going to abolish the Department of Education. When Newt Gingrich and Dick Armey came into control, they said they were going to abolish the Department of Education. Under George W. Bush and the Republican Congress, the budget of that agency has doubled. Jimmy Carter created the Department of Education as a payoff to the teachers unions. The day it was created, the president of the National Education Association said: "Look at us, we are the only special interest group in Washington with our own cabinet agency." That was true: It has become nothing but a sounding board for the teachers union ever since. There is no evidence that the money Washington has spent on education has had any positive on school performance. This is quite disappointing.

Consider the Medicare prescription drug bill—the largest expansion of the federal entitlement state since Lyndon Johnson was in office. The Republicans were supposed to get such programs under control. A party that says it will control entitlement spending should not go out and create a new $8 trillion entitlement program. But that is what the Republicans have done.

However, the thing that has hurt Republicans the most is earmark spending. Over the course of the last ten years we have witnessed a thousandfold increase in the number of earmarked, pork barrel projects in the federal budget. When the Republicans regained Congress, they said they were going to get rid of earmark spending. At the time there were 1,500 such projects—roughly four slices of bacon for every member of Congress. By the time the Republicans were evicted from office in 2006 the number of earmarked, pork barrel spending projects had risen from 1,500 to 15,000—about 40 slices of bacon for every member of Congress.

The public has reacted very negatively to that spending, and the Republicans were put on the "bridge to nowhere." This refers to the infamous project Ted Stevens (R-AK), appropriator, had inserted into a Senate appropriations bill—a bridge to link Ketchum, Alaska, population 60,000, to a small island with a population of 48. The bridge was to be larger and longer than San Francisco's Golden Gate. At a cost of $240 million, it would be cheaper to buy a Learjet for every person on that island than to build the bridge. The "bridge to nowhere" has become a symbol of Republican excess during the current Bush administration.

And then there is New Orleans and the Gulf Coast after Hurricane Katrina struck. Personally I thought this was the low point of the Bush presidency. The federal government mishandled virtually every step of the recovery process. To be fair to George Bush, so did the state government and local governments. This is probably one of the best examples of government ineptitude in response to a disaster. A few nights after Katrina devastated the Gulf Coast, George Bush gave a nationally televised speech in which he told the American public, "We will spend whatever it takes to clean up the mess from Katrina." So Congress started to appropriate more money. The size of the pot just kept getting bigger. The initial appropriation was something like $17 billion, which was followed by another $40 billion, which, by the time it was all over, had grown to something like $120 billion. That money hasn't all been spent, and hopefully it won't all be spent. That $120 billion would calculate out to be $250,000 to $300,000 for every family that lost a home in the storm. That is a lot of money to be spending. It would have been cheaper to write a $250,000 check to every family affected by Katrina than to create this alphabet soup of federal, state, and local agencies. Because the federal government stepped in and because the state spent a lot of money and the localities spent a lot of money, the effect was to crowd out private relief efforts. I would make the case that had the federal government done nothing, the cleanup and recovery after Katrina might have gone a lot smoother than it did under FEMA. FEMA obstructed the relief effort that was supposed to be taking place.

The day after Katrina hit, there were a lot of injured people who needed care. Doctors from all over the region came to New Orleans in a humanitarian effort. A FEMA staffer approached one such doctor who was stitching closed a deep gash on a man's forehead and asked who he was and what he was doing. The doctor said that he was a practicing physician in the state of Kentucky and that he had come to help. The FEMA person told the doctor that since he did not have a license to practice medicine in Louisiana he had to cease and desist. Now that is bureaucratic ineptitude of a new magnitude.

One point I have made many times over in my editorials on Katrina—and it is worth emphasizing so that we don't make this mistake again—is that there is no reason for the federal government to be involved in this sort of national disaster effort. We have had many occasions throughout our history where the federal government's involvement in a disaster was at least as disastrous as Katrina, and then the private sector, the private relief efforts, the charities stepped in and set things right. Atlanta is a good example of this. It was destroyed during the Civil War, but the federal government didn't come in and reconstruct that city: The people of the state of Georgia reconstructed Atlanta. Another example is the great Chicago fire of 1871. The Chicago Civil Aid Society was formed two days after the fire had been put out. The CCAS provided aid to the homeless—food, rebuilding efforts, and so on. Within ten years, Chicago was not just rebuilt, it was rebuilt to a greater splendor than before. And it all had been accomplished through private sector initiative—either private charitable contributions or businessmen trying to make profit. Almost zero federal dollars went into the rebuilding of Chicago. Another example is Galveston, which had been destroyed by floods over 100 years ago. Again almost no federal money was sent into that hurricane-ravaged city. Not only was the city rebuilt, firewalls were constructed to prevent future hurricane damage. It is a great story. In 1906, fires resulting from earthquakes destroyed the entire downtown of San Francisco. Again, with no federal financial input San Francisco was rebuilt.

My question is this: Why do we always turn to Washington first these days? Why, whenever anything goes wrong in America today, do we think the federal government has to fix it?

It is because we have this sickness called entitlement mentality.

Entitlement vs. America

Everyone wants to be successful. We want to advance in our jobs and get higher salaries. We want our investments to do well. Who among us wouldn't be thrilled to get in early on the next Microsoft or Google?

And when w e do succeed—when we get raises or when our investments turn out well—we feel pride in our accomplishments. We know we didn't succeed just by luck or by exploiting other people: We succeeded because we *earned* it.

Yet look at how we perceive those who are *really* successful, people like CEOs and financiers who make huge salaries. Very often, we resent them. When we hear the latest report on CEO salaries, do we focus on the rare skill and incredible work it takes to run a top company? Never. Instead, we complain that the compensation is "excessive."

This resentment of success is a popular cultural topic today. We hear story after story about "income inequality," about how the "gap between rich and poor" is widening, and how bad a thing this is. Many ask how we can live in a society in which some people can purchase multimillion-dollar yachts while others have trouble just paying the rent.

Observe that when people complain about the well-being of the so-called "poor"—the vast majority of whom, by the way, have better food, clothing, health care, and amenities than a king of 300 years ago—it is always the fault of the rich, successful people.

How many times have you heard a commentator, in response to a report on income inequality, chide lower-income people for not working hard enough or smart enough, or for not developing the skills needed to be more productive in a high-tech economy? My guess is—Never.

Take, for example, the much beloved "family farm." Many farmers are losing their jobs and homes and not finding new ones. We don't tell them they need to be more farsighted, and that they need to respond to improvements in farming technology just like buggy-whip makers needed to respond to the advent of the automobile. Instead, we blame rich, evil agribusiness for driving these virtuous small farmers out of their bucolic lifestyle.

Are manufacturing workers losing their jobs because foreign companies are more efficient? We don't tell them that they need to work to gain new skillsets. Instead, we blame evil, rich "outsourcers" who choose to hire foreign laborers willing to work for five times less.

Do families have trouble making ends meet? We don't tell people that they shouldn't have children until they can afford them, or that it is irresponsible not to save up for a rainy day. Instead, we curse the financiers.

Does someone lose all his savings after investing it in a single company? We don't say that he is responsible for choosing where to put his money—that he should diversify, and certainly he should never make an investment he doesn't understand. Instead, we blame the company's leaders or the rich for not giving them a big enough "social safety net."

Indeed, the alleged problem of "income inequality" is *always* the fault of the rich.

The rich are seen as people who hoard "society's" wealth for themselves. Former Democrat House Leader Dick Gephardt called these people "winners of life's lottery." This idea of the rich succeeding at our expense is why we hear the expression that businessmen should "give back" to society, as if they stole something from the rest of us. It is why we hear talk about the poor not getting their "fair share."

I am writing on behalf of the Resented Rich—the successful businessmen and financiers. I myself am a professional investor who has made quite a good living doing it.

I too see the fact that so many Americans are struggling today as a moral problem. But the problem isn't with those who are succeeding, but with those who are struggling. It is not that they are inherently bad people—not at all—but that they have swallowed, and live by, what I call "the entitlement mentality"—a highly immoral, destructive way of life promoted by many of our intellectuals and politicians. If not checked, I strongly believe it will bring this country to its knees.

The Entitlement Mentality

What is the entitlement mentality? Before I give my definition, I want to give you a simple example: welfare.

Consider how welfare works. If you have children you can't afford, you are not responsible for finding a way to take care of them—for example, by working multiple jobs or by finding relatives or friends to help you take care of them. Instead, the government says you are entitled to have your needs met, and it takes other people's hard-earned money and gives it to you. You are entitled to the money not because you did anything to deserve it, but simply because you need it.

This is the essence of the entitlement mentality. The belief that individuals deserve the values necessary to live—such as money, food, housing, employment—simply because they need them.

There are two key elements of the entitlement mentality.

The first is that *needing* things, not earning them, entitles you to them. For example, I pay a fortune in taxes—and a lot of welfare checks in the process. The fact that I earned that money obviously doesn't entitle me to it, but the fact that a single mother needs my money *does* entitle her to it.

The second element of the entitlement mentality is the lack of responsibility it demands. You are not, according to this mentality, responsible for sustaining your own life. To get food on your table, or a well-paying job, or kidney dialysis, you don't need to go out and do anything—you just need to need it, and by that fact "society" owes it to you, which means that other people owe it to you.

A lot of people recognize that this mentality exists in our country, and even if they don't totally oppose it, they acknowledge there are problems with it. But what most people don't realize is that this mentality is incredibly common now—it goes far, far beyond welfare. And, I argue, it is bad and destructive in all these other forms, too.

For example, the entitlement mentality is really common among farmers. This might surprise you since farming is generally thought of as a responsible, hard-working profession. In farming, you often produce your own food, work long hours, and engage in very demanding physical labor. Isn't that the exact opposite of being on welfare?

In many cases, no.

There are many individual farmers that, although they work hard physically, don't make ends meet because they can't compete with big agribusinesses that has more advanced machinery, more efficient methods, and many other attributes that enable them to produce tons of high-quality fruit, vegetables, grain, and meat at low prices. Moreover, these same individual farmers often can't compete with foreign farmers who are willing to work for less money and thus can sell cheaper products.

One response to this—the response many farmers of previous generations took—is to switch jobs. That is, if they can't figure out a way to compete, they can find another job. This is, of course, what people have been doing in our nation for generations: Over 90 percent of Americans used to be farmers; now it is less than 2 percent.

But today many farmers find this option unacceptable. They tell the government that they *need* to be farmers. That is the life they are used to, that is what they want to do: They are *entitled* to be farmers.

So the government, even a "conservative" government, gives them massive subsidies, which are just welfare handouts for farmers. The government passes massive tariffs on many foreign products, jacking up the prices of imported products so that domestic farmers can compete. For example, our government places huge tariffs on imported sugar: We pay a lot more than we need to for sugar, and for everything with sugar in it. Why does the government do this? Because American sugar farmers say they "need" to be farmers, just like their parents and grandparents and great-grandparents. They are entitled to that, and the rest of us are responsible for supplying them with that need.

Another example of the entitlement mentality comes up with the issue of so-called "off shoring" manufacturing jobs. This is the name for when, say, a clothing company decides to set up a clothing plant in Taiwan, not the United States, because the laborers there are willing to work for a lot less.

Just as with farming, one response to this would be to find a new job, which is what a lot of people do. These are rational individuals who understand that a capitalist economy is dynamic, that a job that is in high demand yesterday might not be in high demand today. They switch jobs and develop their skills accordingly. Hopefully, they recognize that every productive person benefits when companies are able to produce clothes, or food, or computers more cheaply. More can be produced, and they will cost less.

Still, there are those parasites who refuse to accept the reality of a changing economy. If they earned $15 an hour 10 years ago to operate a textile machine, they believe they are entitled to earn $25 an hour for the same job today. What about the fact that other people are willing to do that job for less? What about the fact that if their company continues to pay them the same rate, it will be destroyed by foreign competition that can produce the same quality goods for a lot less? What about the fact that other Americans understandably want to buy cheaper clothing?

These folks don't care. They *need* this job, they say, and so they are entitled to it. They are, by the way, encouraged in this mentality by demagogue politicians like John Kerry, who coined the term "Benedict Arnold" CEOs to describe people who use foreign labor.

Let's look at one more industry that you might not think would possess the entitlement mentality, but is full of it: the computer industry.

Historically, this has been known as a highly entrepreneurial industry in which hardworking people earned huge salaries. Back in the late 1990s, when everyone and his grandmother was starting a dot-com business, computer-based skills were in huge demand. Of course, they are still in demand today, but more domestic computer programmers and engineers, plus access to foreign programmers and engineers have made the market for employment as a programmer more competitive.

Just as in other industries, people in the computer industry started complaining about foreign competition, about their companies engaging in "outsourcing" their jobs, as if they are entitled to a certain job at a certain wage, no matter who else has become qualified for that job, or no matter that others are willing to work for less.

Farmers, manufacturing workers, and computer industry workers are examples of a common variant of the entitlement mentality today: the idea that you are entitled to a job—a certain job, in a certain industry, at a certain pay, no matter what. And if you don't get it, you have every right to raise hell with the government, and get them to subsidize you or to punish your competitors.

There are many other examples of the entitlement mentality. Another major category, in addition to job entitlement, is what I call the "right to X" mentality.

You hear the term "right" a lot lately, but the only proper conception of a right is a right to freedom of action. That is, you have a right to free speech—no one can stop you from speaking on your own property. Or you have a right to property: You can do what you want with your property.

But the "right to X" mentality says you have a right to whatever you lack or need, things that must be produced by someone else. Take, for example, the idea of a "right" to health care. In today's America, increasingly the belief is that you have a right to be cured of whatever disease you may get—no matter how expensive the technology, no matter how irresponsible you have been healthwise, no matter how much time it takes doctors to treat you—all paid for at society's expense. The same applies to the "right" to a college education, the right to housing, the right to any other entitlement politicians dream up.

What are the consequences of the entitlement mentality? What does it do to those who have it? What does it do to those who have to pay for it? It is harmful to all. The entitlement mentality is the exact antithesis of the *productive* and *dynamic* culture that made America great.

Step back for a moment and think about how America got to where it is today. How did we, both the rich and the not-so-rich, create so much wealth? It wasn't only our muscle or brute force; it wasn't only our natural resources—of which other countries have much more. In short, America has traditionally been a culture focused on *producing*.

Our history is filled with people who have had *ideas* for new inventions or methods of production, and have put those ideas into action, thus making themselves and others more productive. At the same time, competitors look for opportunities to make themselves more productive. Everyone keeps evolving, growing more productive, and therefore wealthier.

Let's take an example from history: the McCormick Reaper, which was one of the first agricultural tools of the industrial revolution. It was an incredibly efficient way to harvest wheat.

A young Cyrus McCormick saw great value in the reaper and over a number of years invested time and savings to patent, produce, refine, improve, market, demonstrate, and distribute it. He made a lot of money selling it for $100 a unit, which his customers were eager to pay, because it made them far more productive.

Without a McCormick reaper, it took six people a day to harvest two acres of wheat; with one, it took two people a day to harvest ten acres. What of those whose jobs were no longer needed because of the McCormick reaper? They were free to seek new opportunities to produce new goods or services that people had been previously unable to afford because they were spending all their time or money on producing food. Incidentally, these jobs were a lot more appealing to most people, since they didn't have to do backbreaking labor all day.

Here is how the wonder of the McCormick reaper is described by historian Herbert Casson: "Of the ten or twelve sweating drudges who toiled in the harvest-field, all were now to be set free—the sickles, the cradlers, rakers, binders—every one except the driver, and he was to have the glory of riding on the triumphal chariot of a machine that did all the work itself."[1]

All of America's amazing wealth and wonderful progress depends on the kind of productive, dynamic culture that we have had throughout our history. That culture represents the exact opposite of the entitlement mentality. For the McCormick reaper to succeed, everyone needed to embrace the change of progress. This was easy for McCormick's customers, since they clearly stood to be much more productive and profitable. But it was also the case for the wheat harvesters who were temporarily out of a job. If they did not change with the times and find new opportunities, they were left behind. Can you imagine if everyone had the entitlement mentality back at the time of the McCormick Reaper? Ninety percent of us would still be farmers—and America would be just another poor third-world country struggling to feed itself.

Those who have the entitlement mentality—whether in an obvious form, like welfare recipients, or in a less obvious form, like subsidy-and-tariff-receivers—are parasites. They drain and restrict those who produce, grow, and move society ahead.

For example, say you want to start a new software company and hire terrific programmers at the lowest cost. If the anti-outsourcers have their way, you can't do that. The fact that you can hire two Indian programmers for the price of one American programmer, saving time and money for you and your customers, is irrelevant to them. These people believe they are entitled to that job, and they are extracting that entitlement at the cost of your wealth, freedom, and ideas.

We are all familiar with the expansion of our massive entitlement state, with Social Security and Medicare draining vast sums of money from productive people, and with those programs having over $50 trillion in unfunded future liabilities.

I do believe America is full of opportunity, but the entitlement mentality moves us in the wrong direction. It tells people they are not responsible for their own lives and that any needs they might have will be taken care of by "society."

Further, the entitlement mentality creates unhappiness. Self-esteem, which happiness depends on, is the belief that one is worthy and capable of succeeding. That is impossible for someone who knows that they are not coping with life on their own, but rather depending on others to deal with reality for them.

A successful, happy, and prosperous existence requires a life of productivity and growth. The entitlement mentality fosters the exact opposite. It is a danger to the American economy and to the American way of life.

What is the opposite of the entitlement mentality? Let's look at two fields in which the entitlement mentality would never fly: business.

I trade stocks for a living. I enjoy it, I want a job in this field, and I'm used to a certain standard of living. Let's say I make a series of bad trades, that I thought there was an amazing future in Pets.com and invested 50 percent of my clients' money there and ended up losing most of it.

For understandable reasons, many of my clients would then decide to hire someone else to manage their money. Also for understandable reasons, when I tell prospective clients my track record, they decide that another money manager would be a smarter choice.

So I'm out of a job. What if I said, I like being a money manager, I enjoy this job, I'm accustomed to it, I'm used to a certain standard of living—why should I be punished just for making a poor investment? I appeal to Washington to pass the Bad Investors Employment Act, which forces individuals to put some of their money with failed investors like me.

Is that just? Imagine what would happen to the investment world if this mentality took hold.

Of course, it won't. If I make a bad investment, I pay for my mistakes. I own up and tell my clients and prospective clients. I try to give them a *rational* explanation of why it is still in their self-interest to deal with me. Many stick around, but many leave. To that end, maybe I'll have to skimp for a couple of years, investing only a small amount of money, but improving my track record.

If I can't convince anyone to invest with me, I have no option but to leave the field. If I really, really want to get back into investing, I can save my money and start a small fund to try to get back into the game.

Observe that this is the exact opposite of the entitlement mentality. Instead of using need as a means of getting values from other people, in the investment field we offer *values* as a means of getting values from other people; we trade. This the *trader* or the *investment mentality*.

The Trader Mentality

The trader recognizes that nature does not give us our survival for free. This imposes on each of us an obligation to create the values that sustain our lives.

If the trader wants something, he recognizes that it is his responsibility to earn it by producing enough wealth to trade for it.

An aspiring CEO doesn't demand that shareholders give him a job; he appeals to their self-interest to put their company in his trust based on his productivity. His appeal might include his excellent track record or his wealth of innovative ideas. Of course, if he fails, he doesn't tell others that they owe him a living. This success is dependent only insofar as he can *earn* a living in an open, competitive market.

Indeed, in the business world, we expect others to deal with us as *traders*, not *needers*.

For instance, you like your current cell phone company, but get a better offer from another provider. Do you hem and haw about the well-being of Cingular? No, you switch to Verizon.

If Cingular pleaded that they're sorry, but they've had problems in management, human relations, or their communication towers have been falling down, I'm guessing you wouldn't bat an eyelash before picking up your new Verizon phone. You certainly wouldn't demand a "Subsidize Cingular" bill.

Why? Because you recognize that you are not their slave just because they need you. You will deal with them only as long as it's *mutually beneficial*; once it is not, you go your separate ways. If they can't cut it in the cell phone business, too bad. There is no such thing as a right to make a living as a cell phone provider. One has the right to offer products on a free market, but *success* must be *earned*. If Cingular fails to compete, then they deserve to fail.

What if all Americans had the trader mentality? When individuals found themselves in a shrinking field, what if they immediately started developing new skills. What if farmers, when the need for their profession declined, eagerly took up new lines of work?

Can you imagine how fast Americans would come to dominate new industries? Can you imagine how many more small businesses would be started, as individuals tried to create new products and services to appeal to new markets? Can you imagine how productive, satisfying, and dynamic people's lives would be? And can you imagine how much more wealth would be produced—making all of our standards of living higher?

This reality *is* possible. It is the foundation on which this country was built!

This was the once land of "rugged individualism." "Individualism" is a term you hear often, but I doubt that most people have thought about what it means. Fundamentally, it means that the individual, not the group, is what is important and valuable. Groups after all, are only collections of individuals.

Because individuals matter, each individual has to regard others not as serfs to be sacrificed for his benefit or his group's benefit or "society's" benefit, but as people with a right to lead their lives as they choose. To get something from them, he has to *trade* with them.

One example of the trader mentality in American history was the massive immigration in the late nineteenth and early twentieth century. Today there is much resentment about immigrants coming to this country simply to live off welfare checks signed by Uncle Sam. But there was none of this mentality at the turn of the century: For one thing, there was no welfare.

My own family came here in the late 1800s when there was no minimum wage, no government health care, no public schools, or other handouts. They came because they were attracted to America's freedom, and to the idea of being an individual and making their own way. They did not think that the citizens of the nation owed them a living—nor, once they became successful, did they think that they were responsible for feeding and nurturing everyone who claimed to need them.

In America's economic history, rugged individualism has led to wonderful things. Individuals responsible for their own lives were continuously devising ways to make themselves more productive and successful.

Each was free to use his own mind for his own benefit—and if he wanted the products or services of others, he had to *earn* them. Society's general freedom of competition led to continually better, more productive, and more profitable jobs for everyone. Eventually, individuals became so productive that child labor—which had been necessary throughout human history because people were not very productive—became a thing of the past.

So what happened?

Since the founding of this country, we have slowly been moving toward a certain moral idea that contradicted individualism and the trader mentality. We have moved toward a morality that *necessitated*—in fact, *created*—the entitlement mentality.

The name for this ideal is *altruism*: The idea that morality consists of selfless service to others.

Altruism is *incompatible* with individualism. Individualism means your life belongs to *you*, and you can do with it whatever *you* want (so long as you don't violate the rights of others). You have a right to *your* life, *your* liberty, *your* pursuit of happiness.

Altruism is also incompatible with individual liberty. If you take altruism seriously, you cannot be in favor of the kind of nearly laissez-faire capitalist system that our Constitution created—in which individuals are fully free to pursue their own self-interest, regardless of the needs of their neighbors or suffering third-world countries.

Think about it: If the proper way for you to live your life is to be a Mother Theresa, why should you be free to become a rich hedge-fund trader? Maybe the government should let you do that activity, but you certainly shouldn't be able to become rich from it.

What altruism *is* compatible with is a government that forces you to do your duty to serve others—a collectivist government that forces everyone to sacrifice for the group.

This is not just speculation on my part, our history has borne it out. When industrialists in this country started to make huge amounts of money through free trade with others—trade that, by the way, made those they dealt with much better off, which is plainly true from skyrocketing life expectancy figures—intellectuals denounced them as "Robber Barons." Gradually they devised ways to take from them, most notably, by the federal income tax, passed as a Constitutional Amendment in 1913. Over the years, with altruistic justifications, we got welfare, Social Security, Medicare, Medicaid, and so on. These are the institutions that have promoted the entitlement mentality.

Don't get the impression that altruism *inadvertently* caused the entitlement mentality by creating these institutions, which is the view of many conservatives. They think that such programs are noble ideals, but carry "unintended consequences," like a growing sense of entitlement.

The entitlement mentality is part and parcel of altruism. Think about it: If the individual, especially the well-off individual, is morally obligated to sacrifice for the sake of needy others, then the recipient is *entitled* to the sacrifice. It is not just an act of generosity or charity; the giver is doing his *moral duty*. So if you make $100,000 a year, and some woman makes nothing, then altruism says you are *obligated* to sacrifice to her—and she is entitled to your sacrifice.

So anytime she or any other so-called "have-not" can point to something the "haves" have that they don't—great medical care, fancy private schools, nice houses—they can demand it—they are *entitled* to it. And in today's culture, they do.

Observe how this works in today's political climate of pressure-group warfare. Every different group brandishes its needs, and demands that "society"—that is, other people—supply them with what they need. It is impossible to criticize the entitlement mentality, without attacking its basic root: altruism.

Altruism is nothing to aspire to. It is a baseless, destructive, and unjust idea. Why in the world should I be a moral slave to the needs of others? Why should the most productive people be chained to the world's failures? Charity is a perfectly legitimate thing, if you can afford it and if you have a deserving recipient—but the idea that you should give until it hurts to satisfy endless needs around the world is ludicrous.

You can see what it leads to. It rewards failure, laziness, inactivity, stagnation, irresponsibility—it rewards the farmer who wants to do the same work the same way that his ancestors did, but wants to make enough money to afford all the goods produced by the evolving fields of work. It rewards the 22-year-old woman who has promiscuous, un-protected sex with multiple partners, or who chooses to have children because she feels like it at that moment, damn the consequences. And it has no moral concern for the productive people who want to pursue their *personal* happiness by earning it.

If you're going to fight the entitlement mentality, you need to mor-ally oppose the ideal of altruism. You need to step outside the altruist perspective where only the needy matter. The entitlement mentality harms *innocent, productive* people. These are the virtuous people who take responsibility for sustaining their lives, who do so exceptionally well, and who only ask for what they can earn.

We are all traders. We are not born into society to serve "the public"—that is, other people—nor are those other people here to serve us.

As a professional investor, I work in a world where this truth is recognized. For the good of our country, I hope that our society at large starts to recognize it, too.

Note

1. Herbert Casson, *Cyrus Hall McCormick: His Life and Work* (Chicago: McClurg and Co., 1909).

LUDWIG VON MISES

ON EQUALITY AND INEQUALITY

I

The doctrine of natural law that inspired the eighteenth century declarations of the rights of man did not imply the obviously fallacious proposition that all men are biologically equal. It proclaimed that all men are born equal in rights and that this equality cannot be abrogated by any man-made law, that it is inalienable or, more precisely, imprescriptible. Only the deadly foes of individual liberty and self-determination, the champions of totalitarianism, interpreted the principle of equality before the law as derived from an alleged psychical and physiological equality of all men. The French declaration of the rights of the man and the citizen of November 3, 1789, had pronounced that all men are born and remain equal in rights. But, on the eve of the inauguration of the regime of terror, the new declaration that preceded the Constitution of June 24, 1793, proclaimed that all men are equal *par la nature.* From then on this thesis, although manifestly contradicting biological experience, remained one of the dogmas of "leftism." Thus we read in the *Encyclopaedia of the Social Sciences* that "at birth human infants, regardless of their heredity, are as equal as Fords."[1]

From *Money, Method and the Market Process.* Reprinted with permission of the Ludwig von Mises Institute (www.mises.org), Auburn, Alamaba.

However, the fact that men are born unequal in regard to physical and mental capacities cannot be argued away. Some surpass their fellow men in health and vigor, in brain and aptitudes, in energy and resolution and are therefore better fitted for the pursuit of earthly affairs than the rest of mankind—a fact that has also been admitted by Marx. He spoke of "the inequality of individual endowment and therefore productive capacity (*Leistungsfähigkeit*)" as "natural privileges" and of "the unequal individuals (and they would not be different individuals if they were not unequal)."[2] In terms of popular psychological teaching we can say that some have the ability to adjust themselves better than others to the conditions of the struggle for survival. We may therefore—without indulging in any judgment of value—distinguish from this point of view between superior men and inferior men.

History shows that from time immemorial superior men took advantage of their superiority by seizing power and subjugating the masses of inferior men. In the status society there is a hierarchy of castes. On the one hand are the lords who have appropriated to themselves all the land and on the other hand their servants, the liegemen, serfs, and slaves, landless and penniless underlings. The inferiors' duty is to drudge for their masters. The institutions of the society aim at the sole benefit of the ruling minority, the princes, and their retinue, the aristocrats.

Such was by and large the state of affairs in all parts of the world before, as both Marxians and conservatives tell us, "the acquisitiveness of the bourgeoisie," in a process that went on for centuries and is still going on in many parts of the world, undermined the political, social, and economic system of the "good old days." The market economy—capitalism—radically transformed the economic and political organization of mankind.

Permit me to recapitulate some well-known facts. While under precapitalistic conditions superior men were the masters on whom the masses of the inferior had to attend, under capitalism the more gifted and more able have no means to profit from their superiority other than to serve to the best of their abilities the wishes of the majority of the less gifted. In the market economic power is vested in the consumers. They ultimately determine, by their buying or abstention from buying, what should be produced, by whom and how, of what quality and in what quantity. The entrepreneurs, capitalists, and landowners who fail to satisfy in the best possible and cheapest way the most urgent of the not yet satisfied wishes of the consumers are forced to go out of business and forfeit their preferred position. In business offices and in laboratories the keenest minds are busy fructifying the most complex achievements of scientific research for the production of ever better implements and gadgets for people who have no inkling of the theories that make the fabrication of such things possible. The bigger an enterprise is, the more is it forced to adjust its production to the changing whims and fancies of the masses, its masters. The fundamental principle of capitalism is mass production to supply the masses. It is the patronage of the masses that make enterprises grow big. The common man is supreme in the market economy. He is the customer who "is always right."

In the political sphere, representative government is the corollary of the supremacy of the consumers in the market. Office-holders depend on the voters as entrepreneurs and investors depend on the consumers. The same historical process that substituted the capitalistic mode of production for precapitalistic methods substituted popular government—democracy—for royal absolutism and other forms of government by the few. And wherever the market economy is superseded by socialism, autocracy makes a comeback. It does not matter whether the socialist or communist despotism is camouflaged by the use of aliases like "dictatorship of the proletariat" or "people's democracy" or "*Führer* principle." It always amounts to a subjection of the many to the few.

It is hardly possible to misconstrue more thoroughly the state of affairs prevailing in capitalistic society than by calling the capitalists and entrepreneurs a "ruling" class intent upon "exploiting" the masses of decent men. We will not raise the question of how the men who under capitalism are in business would have tried to take advantage of their superior talents in any other thinkable organization of production. Under capitalism they are vying with one another in serving the masses of less gifted men. All their thoughts aim at perfecting the methods of supplying the consumers. Every year, every month, every week something unheard of before appears on the market and is soon made accessible to the many.

What has multiplied the "productivity of labor" is not some degree of effort on the part of manual workers, but the accumulation of capital by the savers and its reasonable employment by the entrepreneurs. Technological inventions would have remained useless trivia if the capital required for their utilization had not been previously accumulated by thrift. Man could not survive as a human being without manual labor. However, what elevates him above the beasts is not manual labor and the performance of routine jobs, but speculation, foresight that provides for the needs of the—always uncertain—future. The characteristic mark of production is that it is behavior directed by the mind. This fact cannot be conjured away by a semantics for which the word "labor" signifies only manual labor.

II

To acquiesce in a philosophy stressing the inborn inequality of men runs counter to many people's feelings. More or less reluctantly, people admit that they do not equal the celebrities of art, literature, and science, at least in their specialties, and that they are no match for athletic champions. But they are not prepared to concede their own inferiority in other human matters and concerns. As they see it, those who outstripped them in the market, the successful entrepreneurs and businessmen, owe their ascendancy exclusively to villainy. They themselves are, thank God, too honest and conscientious to resort to those dishonest methods of conduct that, as they say, alone make a man prosper in a capitalistic environment.

Yet, there is a daily growing branch of literature that blatantly depicts the common man as an inferior type: the books on the behavior of consumers and the alleged evils of advertising.[3] Of course, neither the authors nor the public that acclaims their writings openly state or believe that that is the real meaning of the facts they report.

As these books tell us, the typical American is constitutionally unfit for the performance of the simplest tasks of a householder's daily life. He or she does not buy what is needed for the appropriate conduct of the family's affairs. In their inwrought stupidity they are easily induced by the tricks and wiles of business to buy useless or quite worthless things. For the main concern of business is to profit not by providing the customers with the goods they need, but by unloading on them merchandise they would never take if they could resist the psychological artifices of "Madison Avenue." The innate incurable weakness of the average man's will and intellect makes the shoppers behave like "babes."[4] They are easy prey to the knavery of the hucksters.

Neither the authors nor the readers of these passionate diatribes are aware that their doctrine implies that the majority of the nation are morons, unfit to take care of their own affairs and badly in need of a paternal guardian. They are preoccupied to such an extent with their envy and hatred of successful businessmen that they fail to see how their description of consumers' behavior contradicts all that the "classical" socialist literature used to say about the eminence of the proletarians. These older socialists ascribed to the "people," to the "working and toiling masses," to the "manual workers" all the perfections of intellect and character. In their eyes, the people were not "babes" but the originators of what is great and good in the world, and the builders of a better future for mankind.

It is certainly true that the average common man is in many regards inferior to the average businessman. But this inferiority manifests itself first of all in his limited ability to think, to work, and thereby to contribute more to the joint productive effort of mankind. Most people who satisfactorily operate in routine jobs would be found wanting in any performance requiring a modicum of initiative and reflection. But they are not too dull to manage their family affairs properly. The husbands who are sent by their wives to the supermarket "for a loaf of bread and depart with their arms loaded with their favorite snack items"[5] are certainly not typical. Neither is the housewife who buys regardless of content, because she "likes the package."[6]

It is generally admitted that the average man displays poor taste. Consequently business, entirely dependent on the patronage of the masses of such men, is forced to bring to the market inferior literature and art. (One of the great problems of capitalistic civilization is how to make high quality achievements possible in a social environment in which the "regular fellow" is supreme.) It is furthermore well known that many people indulge in habits that result in undesired effects. As the instigators of the great anti-capitalistic campaign see it, the bad taste and the unsafe consumption habits of people and the other evils of our age are simply generated by the public relations or sales activities of the various branches of "capital"—wars are made by the munitions industries, the "merchants of death"; dipsomania by alcohol capital, the fabulous "whiskey trust," and the breweries.

This philosophy is not only based on the doctrine depicting the common people as guileless suckers who can easily be taken in by the ruses of a race of crafty hucksters. It implies in addition the nonsensical theorem that the sale of articles which the consumer really needs and would buy if not hypnotized by the wiles of the sellers is unprofitable for business and that on the other hand only the sale of articles which are of little or no use for the buyer or are even downright detrimental to him yields large profits. For if one were not to assume this, there would be no reason to conclude that in the competition of the market the sellers of bad articles outstrip those of better articles. The same sophisticated tricks by means of which slick traders are said to convince the buying public can also be used by those offering good and valuable merchandise on the market. But then good and poor articles compete under equal conditions and there is no reason to make a pessimistic judgment on the chances of the better merchandise. While both articles—the good and the bad—would be equally aided by the alleged trickery of the sellers, only the better one enjoys the advantage of being better.

We need not consider all the problems raised by the ample literature on the alleged stupidity of the consumers and their need for protection by a paternal government. What is important here is the fact that, notwithstanding the popular dogma of the equality of all men, the thesis that the common man is unfit to handle the ordinary affairs of his daily life is supported by a great part of popular "leftist" literature.

III

The doctrine of the inborn physiological and mental equality of men logically explains differences between human beings as caused by postnatal influences. It emphasizes especially the role played by education. In the capitalistic society, it is said, higher education is a privilege accessible only to the children of the "bourgeoisie." What is needed is to grant every child access to every school and thus educate everyone.

Guided by this principle, the United States embarked upon the noble experiment of making every boy and girl an educated person. All young men and women were to spend the years from six to eighteen in school, and as many as possible of them were to enter college. Then the intellectual and social division between an educated minority and a majority of people whose education was insufficient was to disappear. Education would no longer be a privilege; it would be the heritage of every citizen.

Statistics show that this program has been put into practice. The number of high schools, of teachers and students multiplied. If the present trend goes on for a few years more, the goal of the reform will be fully attained; every American will graduate from high school.

But the success of this plan is merely apparent. It was made possible only by a policy that, while retaining the name "high school," has entirely destroyed its scholarly and scientific value. The old high school conferred its diplomas only on students who had at least acquired a definite minimum knowledge in some disciplines considered as basic. It eliminated in the lower grades those who lacked the abilities and the disposition to comply with these requirements. But in the new regime of the high school the opportunity to choose the subjects he wished to study was badly misused by stupid or lazy pupils. Not only are fundamental subjects such as elementary arithmetic, geometry, physics, history, and foreign languages avoided by the majority of high school students, but every year boys and girls receive high school diplomas who are deficient in reading and spelling English. It is a very characteristic fact that some universities found it necessary to provide special courses to improve the reading skill of their students. The often passionate debates concerning the high school curriculum that have now been going on for several years prove clearly that only a limited number of teenagers are intellectually and morally fit to profit from school attendance. For the rest of the high school population the years spent in class rooms are simply wasted. If one lowers the scholastic standard of high schools and colleges in order to make it possible for the majority of less gifted and less industrious youths to get diplomas, one merely hurts the minority of those who have the capacity to make use of the teaching.

The experience of the last decades in American education bears out the fact that there are inborn differences in man's intellectual capacities that cannot be eradicated by any effort of education.

IV

The desperate, but hopeless attempts to salvage, in spite of indisputable proofs to the contrary, the thesis of the inborn equality of all men are motivated by a faulty and untenable doctrine concerning popular government and majority rule.

This doctrine tries to justify popular government by referring to the supposed natural equality of all men. Since all men are equal, every individual participates in the genius that enlightened and stimulated the greatest heroes of mankind's intellectual, artistic, and political history. Only adverse postnatal influences prevented the proletarians from equaling the brilliance and the exploits of the greatest men. Therefore, as Trotsky told us,[7] once this abominable system of capitalism will have given way to socialism, "the average human being will rise to the heights of an Aristotle, a Goethe, or a Marx." The voice of the people is the voice of God, it is always right. If dissent arises among men, one must, of course, assume that some of them are mistaken. It is difficult to avoid the inference that it is more likely that the minority errs than the majority. The majority is right, because it is the majority and as such is borne by the "wave of the future."

The supporters of this doctrine must consider any doubt of the intellectual and moral eminence of the masses as an attempt to substitute despotism for representative government.

However, the arguments advanced in favor of representative government by the liberals of the nineteenth century—the much-maligned Manchestermen and champions of laissez faire—have nothing in common with the doctrines of the natural inborn equality of men and the superhuman inspiration of majorities. They are based upon the fact, most lucidly exposed by David Hume, that those at the helm are always a small minority as against the vast majority of those subject to their orders. In this sense every system of government is minority rule and as such can last only as long as it is supported by the belief of those ruled that it is better for themselves to be loyal to the men in office than to try to supplant them by others ready to apply different methods of administration. If this opinion vanishes, the many will rise in rebellion and replace by force the unpopular office-holders and their systems by other men and another system. But the complicated industrial apparatus of modern society could not be preserved under a state of affairs in which the majority's only means of enforcing its will is revolution. The objective of representative government is to avoid the reappearance of such a violent disturbance of the peace and its detrimental effects upon morale, culture, and material well-being. Government by the people, i.e., by elected representatives, makes peaceful change possible. It warrants the agreement of public opinion and the principles according to which the affairs of state are conducted. Majority rule is for those who believe in liberty not as a metaphysical principle, derived from an untenable distortion of biological facts, but as a means of securing the uninterrupted peaceful development of mankind's civilizing effort.

V

The doctrine of the inborn biological equality of all men begot in the nineteenth century a quasi-religious mysticism of the "people" that finally converted it into the dogma of the "common man's" superiority. All men are born equal. But the members of the upper classes have unfortunately been corrupted by the temptation of power and by indulgence in the luxuries they secured for themselves. The evils plaguing mankind are caused by the misdeeds of this foul minority. Once these mischief makers are dispossessed, the inbred nobility of the common man will control human affairs. It will be a delight to live in a world in which the infinite goodness and the cogenital genius of the people will be supreme. Never-dreamt-of happiness for everyone is in store for mankind.

For the Russian Social Revolutionaries this mystique was a substitute for the devotional practices of Russian Orthodoxy. The Marxians felt uneasy about the enthusiastic vagaries of their most dangerous rivals. But Marx's own description of the blissful conditions of the "higher phase of Communist Society"[8] was even more sanguine. After the extermination of the Social-Revolutionaries the Bolsheviks themselves adopted the cult of the common man as the main ideological disguise of their unlimited despotism of a small clique of party bosses.

The characteristic difference between socialism (communism, planning, state capitalism, or whatever other synonym one may prefer) and the market economy (capitalism, private enterprise system, economic freedom) is this: in the market economy the individuals *qua* consumers are supreme and determine by their buying or not-buying what should be produced, while in the socialist economy these matters are fixed by the government. Under capitalism the customer is the man for whose patronage the suppliers are striving and to whom after the sale they say "thank you" and "please come again." Under socialism the "comrade" gets what "big brother" deigns to give him and he is to be thankful for whatever he got. In the capitalistic West the average standard of living is incomparably higher than in the communistic East. But it is a fact that a daily increasing number of people in the capitalistic countries—among them also most of the so-called intellectuals—long for the alleged blessings of government control.

It is vain to explain to these men what the condition of the common man both in his capacity as a producer and in that of a consumer is under a socialist system. An intellectual inferiority of the masses would manifest itself most evidently in their aiming at the abolition of the system in which they themselves are supreme and are served by the elite of the most talented men and in their yearning for the return to a system in which the elite would tread them down.

Let us not fool ourselves. It is not the progress of socialism among the backward nations, those that never surpassed the stage of primitive barbarism and those whose civilizations were arrested many centuries ago, that shows the triumphant advance of the totalitarian creed. It is in our Western circuit that socialism makes the greatest strides. Every project to narrow down what is called the "private sector" of the economic organization is considered as highly beneficial, as progress, and is, if at all, only timidly and bashfully opposed for a short time. We are marching "forward" to the realization of socialism.

VI

The classical liberals of the eighteenth and nineteenth centuries based their optimistic appreciation of mankind's future upon the assumption that the minority of eminent and honest men would always be able to guide by persuasion the majority of inferior people along the way leading to peace and prosperity. They were confident that the elite would always be in a position to prevent the masses from following the pied pipers and demagogues and adopting policies that must end in disaster. We may leave it undecided whether the error of these optimists consisted in overrating the elite or the masses or both. At any rate it is a fact that the immense majority of our contemporaries is fanatically committed to policies that ultimately aim at abolishing the social order in which the most ingenious citizens are impelled to serve the masses in the best possible way. The masses—including those called the intellectuals—passionately advocate a system in which they no longer will be the customers who give the orders but wards of an omnipotent authority. It does not matter that this economic system is sold to the common man under the label "to each according to his needs" and its political and constitutional corollary, unlimited autocracy of self-appointed office-holders, under the label "people's democracy."

In the past, the fanatical propaganda of the socialists and their abettors, the interventionists of all shades of opinion, was still opposed by a few economists, statesmen, and businessmen. But even this often lame and inept defense of the market economy has almost petered out. The strongholds of American snobbism and "patricianship," fashionable, lavishly endowed universities and rich foundations, are today nurseries of "social" radicalism. Millionaires, not "proletarians," were the most efficient instigators of the New Deal and the "progressive" policies it engendered. It is well known that the Russian dictator was welcomed on his first visit to the United States with more cordiality by bankers and presidents of big corporations than by other Americans.

The tenor of the arguments of such "progressive" businessmen runs this way: "I owe the eminent position I occupy in my branch of business to my own efficiency and application. My innate talents, my ardor in acquiring the knowledge needed for the conduct of a big enterprise, my diligence raised me to the top. These personal merits would have secured a leading position for me under any economic system. As the head of an important branch of production I would also have enjoyed an enviable position in a socialist commonwealth. But my daily job under socialism would be much less exhausting and irritating. I would no longer have to live under the fear that a competitor can supersede me by offering something better or cheaper on the market. I would no longer be forced to comply with the whimsical and unreasonable wishes of the consumers. I would give them what I—the expert—think they ought to get. I would exchange the hectic and nerve-wracking job of a business man for the dignified and smooth functioning of a public servant. The style of my life and work would resemble much more the seigniorial deportment of a grandee of the past than that of an ulcer-plagued executive of a modern corporation. Let philosophers bother about the true or alleged defects of socialism. I, from my personal point of view, cannot see any reason why I should oppose it. Administrators of nationalized enterprises in all parts of the world and visiting Russian officials fully agree with my point of view."

There is of course, no more sense in the self deception of these capitalists and entrepreneurs than in the daydreams of the socialists and communists of all varieties.

VII

As ideological trends are today, one has to expect that in a few decades, perhaps even before the ominous year 1984, every country will have adopted the socialist system. The common man will be freed from the tedious job of directing the course of his own life. He will be told by the authorities what to do and what not to do, he will be fed, housed, clothed, educated, and entertained by them. But, first of all, they will release him from the necessity of using his own brains. Everybody will receive "according to his needs." But what the needs of an individual are, will be determined by the authority. As was the case in earlier periods, the superior men will no longer serve the masses, but dominate and rule them.

Yet, this outcome is not inevitable. It is the goal to which the prevailing trends in our contemporary world are leading. But trends can change and hitherto they always have changed. The trend toward socialism too may be replaced by a different one. To accomplish such a change is the task of the rising generation.

Notes

1. Horace Kallen, "Behaviorism," in *Encyclopaedia of the Social Sciences*, vol. 2 (New York: Macmillan, 1930), p. 498.
2. Karl Marx, *Critique of the Social Democratic Program of Gotha* [Letter to Bracke, May 5, 1875] (New York: International Publishers, 1938).
3. For example, John K. Galbraith, *The Affluent Society* (Boston: Houghton Mifflin, 1958).
4. Vance Packard, "Babes in Consumerland," *The Hidden Persuaders* (New York: Cardinal Editions, 1957) pp. 90–97.

5. Ibid., p. 95.

6. Ibid., p. 93.

7. Leon Trotsky, *Literature and Revolution,* R. Strunsky, trans. (London: George Allen and Unwin, 1925), p. 256.

8. Marx, *Critique of the Social Democratic Program of Gotha.*